100
GREAT POTATO RECIPES

100
GREAT POTATO RECIPES

DEALERFIELD

This edition specially printed for Dealerfield Ltd,
Glaisdale Parkway, Glaisdale Drive, Nottingham, NG8 4GA,
by Marshall Cavendish Books, London
(a division of Marshall Cavendish Partworks Ltd).
Copyright © Marshall Cavendish 1996, 1997
This edition first printed 1996
Reprinted 1997

ISBN 1-85927-106-5

British Library Cataloguing in Publication Data:
A catalogue record for this book is available from the British Library
Printed and bound in Italy

CONTENTS

THE POPULAR POTATO

As well as being cheap and plentiful, potatoes are a nutritious and endlessly versatile food. They are filling while being low in calories. They are also a source of minerals and vitamins, especially vitamin C, as well as being rich in essential fibre.

Potatoes can be cooked in a multitude of exciting ways: from side dishes as deliciously different as creamy mash and crunchy chips, to complete dishes ranging from soups and salads to pies, bakes and jacket potatoes.

There are two types of potato: new potatoes that appear at the beginning of the season, also appropriately known as first earlies; and second earlies and maincrop potatoes that are left in the ground until the tubers are fully developed. They are then stored for winter use. New potatoes contain lots of moisture and very little starch, and when cooked have a firm, waxy texture. These potatoes are best eaten whole – steamed or boiled – or cold in salads, although larger

ones also make good chips. The skin of a fresh new potato scrapes off easily, but for maximum flavour just wash them lightly.

Older potatoes contain a great deal of starch, giving them a floury texture when cooked. There are several widely available varieties, some of which suit almost every purpose in the kitchen. The rest are best used specifically for boiling, baking or mashing. Maincrop potatoes are often peeled, but since much of the vitamin and mineral content lies in or just under the skin, it is best to leave them unpeeled unless they are old and blemished or have green patches. These are poisonous and should therefore be removed before cooking.

Potatoes should be carefully stored in a cool, dry, dark and well-ventilated place. They should never be kept in polythene bags. Since the tubers taint easily, they should also be kept away from any strong-smelling foods. For best results, new potatoes should be consumed within two days of purchase. However maincrop potatoes, if stored as recommended, will keep for several weeks.

ROAST POTATOES

SERVES 4 · 15 MINS TO PREPARE
1 HR 25 MINS TOTAL TIME · 180 KCAL PER SERVING
SUITABLE FOR VEGETARIANS

450g/1lb potatoes
vegetable oil
flour, to coat (optional)
fresh herbs (optional)

1 Heat the oven to 180°C/350°F/gas 4. Cover the bottom of an ovenproof dish in a thin layer of oil and place it in the oven. Peel the potatoes, cutting larger ones into halves or quarters so that they cook evenly. If wished, parboil the potatoes in salted water for 3 minutes, then drain well, dry and roll in flour.

2 When the fat is sizzling, but not smoking, remove the dish from the oven and place the potatoes in the fat. Turn the potatoes using two spoons so that all sides are well coated with fat. Add any herbs for extra flavour if wished and place near the top of the oven.

3 An alternative, if you are cooking a joint, is to place the potatoes around the meat in the pan base when the fat from the joint has started to run. Turn the potatoes in the fat then baste them from time to time during cooking.

4 When the potatoes are brown on the outside remove them from the dish and serve. If you have used herbs, discard them.

MASHED POTATOES

SERVES 4 · 20 MINS TO PREPARE
40 MINS TOTAL TIME · 150 KCAL PER SERVING
SUITABLE FOR VEGETARIANS

450g/1lb potatoes
25g/1oz butter
1–2tbls milk

1 Peel the potatoes, cutting any larger ones into halves or quarters so that they cook evenly.

2 Either boil the potatoes in lightly salted water, or steam them in a vegetable steamer for 20 minutes or until they are soft. Drain them if necessary, then dry in the saucepan shaking it over a low heat.

3 Mash with a fork or potato masher, until all the lumps have disappeared. For a very fine texture, you can rub the potatoes through a sieve instead.

4 For creamed potatoes, add the butter and milk to the mashed potato and continue to beat the mixture over a low heat until it is light and fluffy and paler in colour.

VARIATIONS
Drizzle a little olive oil into the creamed potatoes when beating for a richer, Mediterranean flavour. Alternatively, add a couple of teaspoons of horseradish sauce for a hotter taste.

CHIPS

SERVES 6 · 1¹/4 HRS TO PREPARE
1³/4 HRS TOTAL TIME WITH DRYING
295 KCAL PER SERVING · SUITABLE FOR VEGETARIANS

700g/1¹/2lb medium-sized potatoes
oil or fat for frying

1 Peel the potatoes, trim the ends and cut them into 1.2cm/¹/2in thick slices and then again into sticks. Soak them in a bowl of cold water for 30 minutes to draw out some of the excess starch. Drain and wrap the potatoes in a tea towel or in several layers of absorbent kitchen towels. Leave to dry for 20 minutes.

2 In a large pan, heat the oil or fat to 180°C/350°F. If you have no fat thermometer, test the temperature by dropping in one chip. If the temperature is right, it should sink and gently bubble.

3 Fry all the chips in batches cooking them until they are soft but not coloured, for about 5 minutes. Lift out the basket and drain each batch on 2–3 layers of kitchen towels on a plate.

4 Raise the heat of the oil or fat to 200°C/400°F. Lower the basket into the pan and cook each batch of chips once again until they are golden (this will ensure that they are crisp but not soggy). Drain the chips on fresh kitchen towels, keeping the first batch(es) warm in the oven until ready to serve.

SAUTÉ POTATOES

SERVES 4 · 20 MINS TO PREPARE · 55 MINS TOTAL TIME
280 KCAL PER SERVING · SUITABLE FOR VEGETARIANS

450g/1lb waxy potatoes
15–20g/¹/2–³/4oz butter
2–3tbls oil
chopped herbs to garnish (optional)

1 Parboil the potatoes for 5 minutes in salted water, then drain and dry them thoroughly with a tea towel or kitchen towels.

2 Cut each potato across into 6mm/¹/4in slices. Put enough butter and oil in a sauté pan to cover the base to 6mm/¹/4in in depth and place over a low heat.

3 Increase the heat to medium and add enough potatoes to just fill the pan. Cook them for a few seconds. Start to turn the potatoes with a fish slice, and keep turning them regularly.

4 As the potatoes begin to absorb the fat, shake the pan over the heat to prevent them from sticking. When the potatoes are cooked, lift them out with a fish slice allowing excess fat to drain away.

5 Place the potatoes on 2–3 layers of kitchen towels to absorb any extra grease.

6 Slide the potatoes on to a warmed serving dish. Sprinkle with herbs if wished and serve at once.

SALADS & SIDE DISHES

IN ADDITION TO MAKING AN ESSENTIAL INGREDIENT FOR MANY FRESH AND CREATIVE SALADS, POTATOES CAN BE TRANSFORMED INTO A VARIETY OF DELICIOUS ACCOMPANIMENTS FOR ALL YOUR FAMILY'S MEALS.

POTATO & PEPPER SALAD

THIS TASTY SALAD IS A GOOD
ACCOMPANIMENT TO GRILLED OR BARBECUED
STEAKS, LAMB CHOPS AND CHICKEN
SERVES 4–6 · 30 MINS TO PREPARE
2¼ HRS TOTAL TIME WITH COOLING
190 KCAL PER SERVING
SUITABLE FOR VEGETARIANS

450g/1lb small new potatoes, scrubbed
1 green pepper
salt
2 celery sticks, diced
1 onion, finely chopped
¹/2 cucumber, peeled and diced
celery leaves, to garnish

DRESSING
150ml/¹/4pt sour cream
1tsp French mustard
pinch of cayenne pepper

1 Cook the potatoes in boiling salted water for 15 minutes, until just tender. Drain and leave to cool completely. Deseed the green pepper, slice off a few rings and reserve for the granish. Dice the rest of the pepper.

2 Combine the green pepper, celery, onion and cucumber together in a salad bowl. Cut the potatoes in half and add them to the salad bowl of vegetables. For convenience, all the vegetables may be prepared a few hours ahead – cover the bowl and refrigerate until required.

3 Just before serving, make the dressing: put the cream in a bowl with the mustard, cayenne pepper and 1 teaspoon salt. Mix well. Pour the dressing over the salad and toss together. Garnish the salad with the reserved pepper rings and a few celery leaves and serve.

VARIATIONS
As a quick alternative, use drained canned new potatoes instead of fresh. To give the dressing a milder flavour, use American mustard instead of French. To serve the salad as a light supper dish, add 100g/4oz chopped ham at step 2.

VEGETABLE SALAD & PEANUT SAUCE

SERVES 4–6 · 30 MINS TO PREPARE
40 MINS TOTAL TIME · 400 KCAL PER SERVING

2 shallots, chopped
1 garlic clove, chopped
3–4 fresh red chillies, deseeded
2tbls vegetable oil
1tsp shrimp paste
100g/4oz peanut butter
300ml/¹/2pt coconut milk
1tbls brown sugar
salt
1tbls lime juice

100g/4oz French beans, topped and tailed
1 large potato, sliced
100g/4oz cauliflower florets
100g/4oz bean sprouts
oil for stir-frying
lettuce leaves
2 eggs, hard-boiled, shelled and quartered
fried onion rings

1 Pound the shallots, garlic and chillies to a coarse pulp. Heat the oil in a wok, stir in the pulp and fry gently for about 2 minutes. Add the shrimp paste, peanut butter, coconut milk, sugar and salt to taste. Bring to the boil, stirring constantly, then add the lime juice. Simmer for 1 minute. Keep the sauce warm.

2 Blanch the beans, potato and cauliflower for 2 minutes in boiling water. Drain. Stir-fry the bean sprouts with a little hot oil in a heavy-based frying pan over high heat for 1 minute. Line a large plate with lettuce leaves and arrange the vegetables on top. Pour over the peanut sauce. Add the eggs and onion rings and serve warm.

WHAT TO DRINK
This dish of warm, comforting potatoes with a brush of acidity from the gherkins would go well with a glass of New Zealand Sauvignon Blanc.

VARIATIONS
Add chunks of tuna to this potato salad to turn it into a substantial main course dish. If parsley is not available, garnish it with chopped capers and anchovies.

WARM POTATO SALAD WITH GHERKINS

WARM POTATOES, COMBINED WITH THE SHARP TANG OF GHERKINS, CREATE A TASTY SALAD DISH TO SERVE AT A SUMMER BUFFET OR AS A WINTER SIDE DISH AT LUNCH

SERVES 4 · 20 MINS TO PREPARE
45 MINS TOTAL TIME · 430 KCAL PER SERVING
SUITABLE FOR VEGETARIANS

700g/1¹/2lb small, even-sized potatoes, preferably new
2 eggs, hard-boiled and shelled
2 large or 6 small pickled gherkins
3tbls fresh chopped parsley

VINAIGRETTE DRESSING
1 large garlic clove, finely chopped
salt
2tbls red or white wine vinegar
¹/2tsp mustard powder
freshly ground black pepper
8tbls olive oil
few sprigs of tarragon, finely chopped (optional)

1 Scrub the potatoes and put them in a saucepan. Cover with cold water, bring to the boil and simmer for about 20 minutes or until tender. Meanwhile, chop the hard-boiled eggs and gherkins into 6mm/¹/4in cubes.

2 To make the vinaigrette: sprinkle a little salt over the garlic and crush to a paste with the flat side of a knife blade. Put in a small bowl. Add the vinegar, mustard powder and pepper, and whisk until blended. Gradually add the olive oil, whisking constantly until well blended and slightly thickened. Stir in the chopped tarragon, if wished.

3 When the potatoes are cooked, drain them and as soon as they are cool enough to handle, peel off the skins using a sharp kitchen knife. Chop them into 20mm/³/4in cubes. Put the potatoes in a bowl and pour the salad dressing over them while they are still warm. Add the chopped egg, gherkin and parsley and toss well. Serve at once.

COOK'S TIPS
To get the best flavour if you wish to serve this salad cold, dress the potatoes while they are still hot as in step 3, but leave to cool before adding the remaining ingredients.

CREAMY POTATO SALAD

SERVES 4 · 15 MINS TO PREPARE · 1 HR 20 MINS TOTAL TIME
WITH COOLING · 240 KCAL PER SERVING
SUITABLE FOR VEGETARIANS

700g/1¹/2lb potatoes, scrubbed
salt
4–8 spring onion tassels, to garnish (optional)
1tbls chopped fresh mint, to garnish (optional)

DRESSING
150ml/¹/4pt sour cream
2tbls capers, rinsed and drained
4 spring onions, thinly sliced
¹/2tsp lemon juice
freshly ground black pepper

1 Bring the potatoes to the boil in salted water and simmer for 15–20 minutes, or until just tender. Meanwhile, prepare the spring onion tassels (see Preparation tip above right) and leave them to curl in a bowl of iced water for at least 30 minutes.

2 Make the dressing: mix all the ingredients together in a bowl with salt and pepper to taste. Drain the potatoes, leave until cool enough to handle, then remove the skins and dice the flesh. Toss the potatoes in the dressing while they are still warm, then leave them to cool completely. Serve the potato salad when it has just cooled and garnish with spring onion tassels and chopped mint.

POTATO & PRAWN SALAD

SERVES 4 · 30 MINS TO PREPARE · 1 HR 50 MINS TOTAL TIME
WITH COOLING · 275 KCAL PER SERVING

450g/1lb waxy new potatoes
salt and freshly ground black pepper
3tbls mayonnaise
¹/2tsp dried tarragon
2 eggs, hard-boiled, shelled and chopped
100g/4oz peeled cooked prawns, defrosted if frozen
7.5cm/3in piece of cucumber, thinly sliced, to garnish

1 Drop the potatoes into salted boiling water and simmer for 15–20 minutes or until tender. Drain, peel and chop, then mix with the mayonnaise, tarragon and salt and pepper to taste. Leave to cool for about 1 hour.

2 Mix the potatoes with the chopped eggs and prawns. Spoon onto a serving dish or four individual plates, surround with the sliced cucumber and serve.

PREPARATION

To prepare a spring onion tassel: trim off the roots, peel off the thin outer skin and cut off most of the green top. Using a very sharp knife, cut several slits close together from the top of the onion down to within about 2.5cm/1in of the bottom of the bulb. Repeat with the remaining onions.

POTATO & RADISH CRUNCH

A FRESH-TASTING SALAD PERFECT
FOR A SUMMER PICNIC OR AS A LIGHT
MEAL ON ITS OWN
SERVES 4 · 30 MINS TO PREPARE
2¹/2 HRS TOTAL TIME WITH COOLING
310 KCAL PER SERVING
SUITABLE FOR VEGETARIANS

450g/1lb new potatoes
salt
50g/2oz butter
3 thick slices white bread, crusts removed
and cut into 1cm/¹/2in dice
5cm/2in piece of cucumber, diced
6 radishes, thinly sliced
25g/1oz dry roasted peanuts
1tsp snipped chives
freshly ground black pepper
4tbls sour cream

1 Bring a saucepan of salted water to the boil and cook the potatoes for 15–20 minutes until just tender. Drain well and, when cool enough to handle, cut into 1cm/¹/2in dice. Leave to cool completely.

2 To make the croûtons: melt the butter in a frying pan. When it is sizzling, add the diced bread and fry gently, turning as necessary, until golden. Drain well on kitchen towels. Leave to cool completely.

3 Place the diced potatoes, fried croûtons, cucumber, radishes, peanuts and chives into a bowl. Season with salt and pepper to taste. Add the sour cream and mix gently. Serve at once.

VARIATIONS

Add a small chopped green pepper instead of cucumber. Omit the peanuts and sprinkle the top of the salad with toasted, flaked almonds.

INGREDIENTS GUIDE

Choose a waxy type of potato such as Pentland Javelin or Ulster Sceptre which will not break up during cooking.

COOK'S TIPS

Watch the potatoes carefully: they should be cooked through but still firm. If overcooked, they will break up instead of cutting into neat dice. Mix gently so that the ingredients are thoroughly coated in the sour cream but remain separate.

PIMENTO SALAD

SERVES 4 · 45 MINS TO PREPARE
5 HRS TOTAL TIME WITH CHILLING
285 KCAL PER SERVING · SUITABLE FOR VEGETARIANS

560g/1 1/4lb new potatoes, scrubbed
salt
150ml/1/4pt vinaigrette
2 large tomatoes, halved and deseeded
1 garlic clove
225ml/8fl oz mayonnaise
100g/4oz tinned pimentos, chopped, liquid reserved
1–2tsp paprika, plus extra to sprinkle over salad
1/2 lettuce, washed and dried
1 hard-boiled egg yolk, sieved
watercress, to garnish

1 Boil the potatoes for 15–20 minutes until tender but firm. Drain them, remove the skins and dice. Toss in the vinaigrette and chill for 2 hours. Chill the tomato halves.

2 Meanwhile, crush the garlic to a smooth paste with a little salt and mix into the mayonnaise. Reserve 2 tablespoons. Add the pimentos, their liquid, and the paprika to the remainder of the mayonnaise. Stir until blended. Toss the cold potatoes in the flavoured mayonnaise and chill for a further two hours.

3 Line serving plates with the lettuce leaves and pile on the potato salad. Fill the tomato halves with the reserved mayonnaise and sprinkle with the egg yolk. Arrange the tomatoes and watercress around the dishes. Sprinkle the potato salad with paprika just before serving.

BELGIAN WARM SALAD

SERVES 4–6 · 30 MINS TO PREPARE
55 MINS TOTAL TIME · 310 KCAL PER SERVING

350g/12oz new potatoes, washed
salt
350g/12oz green beans
25g/1oz butter
225g/8oz streaky bacon, cut into fine strips
1 Spanish onion, finely chopped
4tbls wine vinegar
freshly ground black pepper
2tbls finely chopped fresh parsley

1 Boil the potatoes in salted water for 15–20 minutes, until tender. Meanwhile, top and tail the beans and boil in salted water for 8–10 minutes, until tender. Drain the beans and keep warm.

2 Drain the potatoes. Cool slightly and peel, then cut into 6mm/1/4in slices. Keep warm. Meanwhile, melt the butter in a frying pan. Sauté the bacon strips and onion over a high heat until lightly golden, tossing the mixture frequently. Reduce the heat. Pour in the wine vinegar and simmer over a low heat for 3 minutes, stirring occasionally. Season with black pepper to taste.

3 In a salad bowl, combine the drained beans and sliced new potatoes. Pour over the bacon dressing and toss gently until well mixed, taking care not to break up the potato slices. Correct the seasoning, sprinkle with finely chopped parsley and serve at room temperature.

HOT POTATO & PEANUT SALAD

SERVES 4 · 30 MINS TO PREPARE
50 MINS TOTAL TIME · 590 KCAL PER SERVING
SUITABLE FOR VEGETARIANS

700g/1¹/2lb potatoes, cut
   into even-sized pieces
salt
250g/9oz salted peanuts,
   roughly chopped
about 150ml/¹/4pt milk
50g/2oz Cheddar cheese,
   grated
1 small green chilli, or
   ¹/2–1tsp chilli powder

freshly ground black
   pepper
1 lettuce, leaves
   separated

GARNISH
2 tomatoes, sliced
1 onion, sliced into rings
watercress sprigs

1 Boil the potatoes in salted water, for 20 minutes until tender. Meanwhile, reserve 25g/1oz peanuts and put the rest with 150ml/¹/4pt of milk into a blender. Purée until smooth and stir in the grated cheese. Drain the potatoes thoroughly.

2 Wash the chilli and remove the seeds. Rinse under cold running water, then chop finely and add to peanut mixture. Season with salt and pepper to taste.

3 To serve, line a serving dish with lettuce leaves, pile the potatoes into the centre and pour the sauce over the top. Sprinkle with reserved peanuts. Garnish with tomato slices, onion rings and watercress sprigs.

CURRIED POTATO SALAD

SERVES 4 · 30 MINS TO PREPARE · 2 HRS 15 MINS TOTAL TIME
WITH COOLING · 295 KCAL PER SERVING

450g/1lb small new
   potatoes
salt
1¹/2tsp cider vinegar
freshly ground black
   pepper
150ml/¹/4pt sour cream
70ml/3fl oz mayonnaise
1–2tsp curry powder

2tsp lemon juice
2 apples, peeled, cored
   and diced
2 celery sticks, sliced
2 rashers cooked bacon,
   chopped
1 celery stick, to garnish
   (optional)

1 Scrub the potatoes well but do not peel them. Bring a saucepan of salted water to the boil, add the potatoes and boil them for 15–20 minutes, or until just tender. Drain and leave until cool enough to handle. Peel them with a sharp knife, then slice them. Toss the potatoes gently with the vinegar and season with salt and pepper to taste. Leave until cold.

2 In a bowl, combine the sour cream, mayonnaise, curry powder and lemon juice. Mix well. Add the apple, celery and bacon to the potato slices, and pour over the sour cream and curry mixture. Use two spoons to toss the salad well, taking care not to break up the potatoes. Spoon the salad into a serving dish, garnish with the celery stick and chill for at least 1 hour before serving.

1 Put the unpeeled potatoes into a large pan of boiling salted water and return the water to the boil. Then lower the heat and simmer for 10 minutes or until the potatoes are tender.

2 When the potatoes are cooked, turn off the heat and add the frankfurters. Cover and set aside; the frankfurters will be warmed through by the time you have made the dressing.

3 Meanwhile, make the dressing. Mix together the onion, mayonnaise, sour cream, paprika, tarragon and chives, reserving 1 teaspoon of chives for garnish. Season with salt and pepper to taste.

4 Drain the potatoes and frankfurters and gently fold them into the dressing trying not to break them up. Turn into a serving dish and sprinkle with the reserved chives. Serve while still warm.

HOT FRANKFURTER & POTATO SALAD

NEW POTATOES ARE MIXED WITH TASTY FRANKFURTER SAUSAGES AND SMOTHERED IN A CREAMY TARRAGON AND CHIVE DRESSING
SERVES 4 · 15 MINS TO PREPARE · 30 MINS TOTAL TIME
495 KCAL PER SERVING

700g/1¹/2lb new potatoes, halved
salt and and freshly ground black pepper
8–10 frankfurters,
  cut into 4cm/1¹/2in lengths
¹/2 onion, finely chopped
3tbls mayonnaise
150ml/¹/4pt sour cream
2tsp paprika
1tbls chopped fresh tarragon
2tbls snipped fresh chives

SERVING SUGGESTIONS

This salad needs little in the way of accompaniment since it's very filling. Serve it warm with, perhaps, a simple salad of mixed green leaves or a sliced tomato salad, and some crusty bread for very hungry eaters.

INGREDIENTS GUIDE

For this recipe, you can use either frankfurters or American-style hot dogs. Both are usually available in tins as well as in sealed plastic packets — if you use the tinned variety, make sure you drain the sausages well before use.

WHAT TO DRINK

A dry white wine would be a good match for this hot salad. Why not try a German wine, such as Trocken?

DUCHESSE POTATOES

SERVES 4 · 30 MINS TO PREPARE · 1 HR 5 MINS TOTAL TIME
215 KCAL PER SERVING · SUITABLE FOR VEGETARIANS

450g/1lb potatoes, peeled and thickly sliced
salt
15–25g/¹/2–1oz butter
1 large egg
1 large egg yolk
freshly ground black pepper
freshly grated nutmeg
olive oil
1 large egg beaten with 1tbls milk to glaze

1 Heat the oven to 200°C/400°F/gas 6. Cook the potatoes, covered, in simmering salted water for 10 minutes, or until tender. Drain well; return the potatoes to the pan and dry them by shaking the pan over the heat.

2 Rub the potatoes through a fine sieve, or press them through a ricer. Add the butter while the potatoes are warm, and beat with a wooden spoon until the mixture is very smooth. Combine the egg and egg yolk then beat them gradually into the potato mixture. Season with salt, pepper and nutmeg. Beat the mixture until it is fluffy.

3 Lightly oil a baking sheet. Spoon the potato mixture into a piping bag fitted with a 10mm/¹/2in star nozzle and pipe in rosettes on to the baking sheet. Brush the potato with the beaten egg and milk glaze. Bake in the oven for 20–25 minutes or until golden.

POMMES ANNA

SERVES 4 · 30 MINS TO PREPARE · 1¹/4 HRS TOTAL TIME
325 KCAL PER SERVING · SUITABLE FOR VEGETARIANS

700g/1¹/2lb floury potatoes
100g/4oz butter
2 garlic cloves
salt and freshly ground black pepper

1 Heat the oven to 200°C/400°F/gas 6. Peel and slice the potatoes thinly. Butter a large ovenproof dish and cover the base with overlapping slices of potato.

2 Peel and finely chop the garlic. Season the potato slices in the dish generously and sprinkle on a little garlic. Melt the butter and pour a little over the potatoes.

3 Continue with similar layers of potato, garlic, seasoning and butter until all the potato has been used. Cover the dish with foil and bake for 45 minutes.

FREEZER FACTS
It is possible to freeze Pommes Anna. Divide the recipe between two foil freezer dishes at step 1 and continue as above. When cool, over-wrap the dishes with foil or heavy-duty polythene, label and freeze. Store for up to 1 month. To serve, bake in the oven at 190°C/375°F/gas 5 for 45 minutes (there is no need to thaw first). When reheated, transfer the Pommes Anna carefully to a warm serving dish. Serve at once.

POTATO GRATIN

GRATIN À LA
DAUPHINOISE IS ONE OF
THE CLASSIC DISHES OF
FRENCH COOKERY
AND MAKES A WARMING
ACCOMPANIMENT FOR A
WINTER SUPPER
SERVES 4
15 MINS TO PREPARE
1³/4 HRS TOTAL TIME
420 KCAL PER SERVING
SUITABLE FOR VEGETARIANS

4 large potatoes
3 eggs, well beaten
425ml/³/4pt double cream
50g/2oz Gruyère cheese,
  grated
50g/2oz Parmesan cheese,
  grated
salt and freshly ground black
  pepper
pinch of grated nutmeg

TOPPING
50g/2oz Gruyère cheese,
  grated
25g/1oz butter, diced

1 Heat the oven to 150°C/300°F/gas 2. Slice the potatoes to 6mm/¹/4in thick. In a large mixing bowl, beat the eggs with the double cream, then beat in the grated Gruyère and Parmesan. Season with salt, pepper and nutmeg to taste.

2 Add the sliced potatoes to the cream, egg and cheese mixture and mix again until the potato slices are evenly covered.

3 Pour the potato, cream and egg mixture into a buttered 28 x 20cm/11 x 8in gratin dish. Sprinkle the top with the grated Gruyère, dot with diced butter and cook in the oven for 1¹/4–1¹/2 hours or until the potatoes are tender. Serve at once.

TRADITIONAL CHAMP

THIS CLASSIC IRISH DISH OF POTATOES
MASHED WITH LEEKS AND
SERVED WITH LASHINGS OF MELTED
BUTTER MAKES AN IDEAL
ACCOMPANIMENT TO GRILLED GAMMON
SERVES 4 · 15 MINS TO PREPARE · 40 MINS TOTAL TIME
395 KCALS PER SERVING · SUITABLE FOR VEGETARIANS

75g/3oz butter
125ml/4fl oz milk
2 leeks, chopped
6–8 potatoes, cut into even-sized pieces
salt
freshly ground black pepper

1 Put 25g/1oz butter and the milk in a frying pan over medium heat. Stir until the butter melts and add the leeks. Reduce the heat to low and cook for 10–15 minutes or until the leeks are soft, stirring occasionally.

2 Meanwhile, put the potatoes in a large pan of salted water and bring to the boil. Cover and simmer for 20 minutes or until soft when tested with a fork. Drain well.

3 Add the cooked leeks and their cooking liquid to the potatoes and beat until the potatoes are well blended and creamy. Season with salt and pepper to taste.

4 Spoon the potato mixture into a warmed serving dish and make a small well in the centre. Add the remaining butter and serve at once.

VARIATIONS

If you prefer, you could substitute spring onions for the leeks in this recipe – 10–12 spring onions, chopped, would be enough.
To make colcannon, another traditional Irish dish, add 450g/1lb green cabbage, cooked in water and roughly chopped, to the potato and leek mixture at the end of step 3.

WHAT TO DRINK

Try a crisp, country white wine from France with this vegetable dish; a Vin de Pays des Côtes de Gascogne would be ideal for the occasion.

NUTRITION NOTES

The potatoes and leeks used in this dish both give useful amounts of both fibre and vitamin C.

CHALET POTATOES

THESE POTATOES ARE DELICIOUS WITH
ROAST LAMB OR BEEF
SERVES 4 · 15 MINS TO PREPARE
1¼ HRS TOTAL TIME · 355 KCAL PER SERVING
SUITABLE FOR VEGETARIANS

**850g–900g/1³/4–2lb evenly-shaped potatoes, about
6.5cm/2¹/2in long
salt
300ml/¹/2pt double cream
2tsp snipped chives
freshly ground black pepper
sweet paprika
75g/3oz Gruyère or Emmental cheese, grated
1tbls finely chopped fresh parsley
butter, for greasing**

1 Heat the oven to 190°C/375°F/gas 5. Bring the potatoes to the boil in salted water, lower the heat and cook for 5 minutes. Drain well.

2 Grease a round ovenproof dish, about 18cm/7in in diameter and 7.5cm/3in deep. Arrange the potatoes in the dish, standing upright and packed firmly together so that they cannot move.

3 Put the cream in a bowl, stir in the chives and season to taste with black pepper and paprika. Pour into the prepared dish of potatoes.

4 Sprinkle the cheese over the top, to cover the potatoes completely, then bake in the oven for about 1 hour or until the potatoes are cooked through and the cheese is golden.

5 Sprinkle the dish with the chopped fresh parsley and serve pipping hot taking care to lift each potato out whole, with its crusty topping still in place.

VARIATIONS

Omit the chives and season the cream with a little extra paprika before pouring over the potatoes. Use grated Edam or Cheddar cheese for the topping.

COOK'S TIPS

This is an ideal way to serve potatoes for a dinner party or special occasion, as once the dish is in the oven it can simply be left to cook.

OVEN-BAKED
NEW POTATOES

SERVES 4 · 5 MINS TO PREPARE · 1 HR TOTAL TIME
205 KCAL PER SERVING · SUITABLE FOR VEGETARIANS

700g/1¹/2lb small new
  potatoes
4 sprigs of mint
4 sprigs of parsley
salt and freshly ground
  black pepper

25g/1oz butter
1tbls chopped fresh mint
  or 1tsp dried mint
1tbls chopped fresh
  parsley

1 Heat the oven to 180°C/350°F/gas 4. Put the potatoes in a 1.5L/2¹/2pt casserole. Tuck the mint and parsley sprigs amongst the potatoes and season with salt and pepper. Dot the butter over the top.

2 Cover the casserole and bake in the oven for 45–60 minutes until the potatoes are tender when pierced with a fine skewer. Using two spoons, turn the potatoes until evenly coated with the melted butter. Sprinkle with the chopped mint and parsley and serve at once.

COOK'S TIPS

Peeling new potatoes is very time-consuming and not necessary: all they need is a good scrub with a brush to remove any earth. Cook the potatoes when you are using the oven at the same temperature for another dish.

NEW POTATOES & PEAS
IN VELOUTÉ SAUCE

SERVES 4 · 20 MINS TO PREPARE · 55 MINS TOTAL TIME
295 KCAL PER SERVING · SUITABLE FOR VEGETARIANS

700g/1¹/2lb new potatoes
225g/8oz frozen peas
salt

VELOUTÉ SAUCE
20g/1¹/2 oz butter
2tbls flour
175ml/³/4pt chicken stock

175ml/³/4pt milk
freshly ground black
  pepper
pinch of grated nutmeg
2tbls double cream
  (optional)

1 Boil the potatoes for 15 minutes in salted water, or until just tender. Drain, then peel using a sharp knife. Keep warm. Meanwhile, boil the peas in salted water for 3 minutes, or until just tender. Drain well and keep warm.

2 To make the sauce: melt the butter in a small, heavy saucepan. Add the flour and stir over a low heat for 2–3 minutes, to make a pale roux. Bring the stock to the boil separately, then gradually pour it onto the roux, stirring with a wire whisk to prevent lumps from forming. Add the milk, stirring until well blended. Simmer, stirring occasionally, for 10–15 minutes, until the sauce is thick and creamy. Season with salt, pepper and nutmeg to taste. Stir in the cream, if using.

3 Put the potatoes and peas in a heated serving dish and mix thoroughly but lightly. Pour the sauce over the vegetable mixture and serve at once.

FOIL-BAKED NEW POTATOES

NEW POTATOES BAKED IN THIS WAY ARE
PERMEATED WITH A MARVELLOUS
CONCENTRATION OF FLAVOUR AND AROMA
SERVES 4 · 15 MINS TO PREPARE
1¼ HRS TOTAL TIME
205 KCAL PER SERVING
SUITABLE FOR VEGETARIANS

600g/1¼lb small new potatoes
20–24 fresh mint leaves
coarse salt
freshly ground black pepper
50g/2oz butter
sprigs of fresh mint to garnish

1 Heat the oven to 190°C/375°F/gas 5. Wash and dry the potatoes. Divide them between 4 individual squares of foil, large enough to enclose them completely.

2 Bury the mint leaves among the potatoes. Season with coarse salt and freshly ground black pepper to taste, and dot each parcel with 15g/½oz butter.

3 Seal the potatoes tightly in the foil. Lay the parcels, with the join upwards, on a baking sheet and cook for 1 hour. Open up one of the parcels and check if the potatoes are cooked by piercing with a sharp knife. Undo the parcels at the table and garnish with fresh mint.

VARIATIONS
You can also try them baked
with a sprig of fresh dill
instead of the mint.

NEW POTATOES & FENNEL

THIS DISH MAKES THE PERFECT
ACCOMPANIMENT TO GRILLED TROUT,
POACHED SALMON OR WHITE FISH BAKED IN
WINE. FENNEL ALSO COMBINES WELL
WITH CHICKEN
SERVES 4–6 · 15 MINS TO PREPARE
55 MINS TOTAL TIME · 330 KCAL PER SERVING
SUITABLE FOR VEGETARIANS

900g/2lb small new potatoes
75g/3oz butter
1/2tsp sweet paprika
1 small fennel bulb
2 sprigs fresh mint, finely chopped
extra mint springs, to garnish

1 Heat the oven to 180°C/350°F/gas 4. Wash the potatoes and pat dry with a tea towel.

2 Melt the butter over a low heat in a flameproof casserole. Stir in the paprika, then add the potatoes. Using a wooden spoon, turn the potatoes in the butter for about 4 minutes until they are beginning to turn brown on all sides. Cover the casserole with a lid and bake in the oven for 25 minutes.

3 Meanwhile, trim the fennel, reserving the feathery leaves for the garnish. Finely chop the fennel bulb and mix with the chopped mint. If you prefer a milder flavour, use 3 tablespoons chopped fennel leaves instead of the actual bulb.

4 Remove the potatoes from the oven, add the fennel and mint and mix together gently. Cover, return to the oven and continue to cook for a further 15 minutes.

5 Remove the casserole from the oven and stir the potatoes carefully. Garnish them with the reserved fennel leaves and mint sprigs. Serve at once.

YANNI'S LEMON POTATOES

LEMON IS A FAVOURITE FLAVOURING IN GREECE, AND THESE POTATOES BRING WITH THEM A TASTE OF THE MEDITERRANEAN

SERVES 4 · 10 MINS TO PREPARE
50 MINS TOTAL TIME
260 KCAL PER SERVING
SUITABLE FOR VEGETARIANS

900g/2lb even, medium-sized potatoes
juice and grated zest of 1 lemon
salt and freshly ground black pepper
50g/2oz butter
lemon twists, to garnish

1 Heat the oven to 190°C/375°F/gas 5. Peel the potatoes and cut them into thick slices. Place the cut potatoes in a gratin dish and sprinkle with the grated lemon zest and half the juice. Season generously with salt and freshly ground black pepper. Dot the butter over the surface and bake for 15 minutes.

2 Drain the excess fat from the dish and sprinkle the potatoes with the remaining lemon juice. Toss the potatoes and bake for a further 20–25 minutes or until they are golden brown and tender.

3 Transfer the potatoes to a heated serving dish using a slotted spoon. Garnish them with lemon twists and serve at once.

CREAMY MUSTARD POTATOES

SERVES 4 · 15 MINS TO PREPARE · 30 MINS TOTAL TIME
205 KCAL PER SERVING · SUITABLE FOR VEGETARIANS

700g/1 1/2lb new potatoes
salt
2 mint sprigs
1tbls chopped fresh mint and 1 mint spring, to garnish

MUSTARD DRESSING
150g/5oz natural yogurt or sour cream
1tbls grainy mustard
1tsp French mustard
1tsp clear honey
1tbls sunflower oil
freshly ground black pepper

1 Boil the potatoes in salted water with the mint sprigs for about 15 minutes until tender but still firm. Meanwhile, make the mustard dressing: stir together the yogurt or sour cream, mustards, honey and sunflower oil in a small saucepan. Season with pepper to taste, then heat through gently, stirring. Do not allow to boil.

2 Drain the potatoes thoroughly and transfer to a warmed serving dish. Pour the heated sauce over the potatoes and garnish with the chopped mint and whole sprig of mint. Serve at once.

SWISS POTATO RÖSTI

THIS FRIED POTATO
DISH FROM
SWITZERLAND,
PROUNOUNCED
'ROSH-TEE', MAKES
A GREAT
COMPLEMENT TO ALL
MEAT DISHES OR CAN
BE SERVED WITH A
SIMPLE SALAD FOR
SUPPER
SERVES 4-6
20 MINS TO PREPARE
1 HR 10 MINS TOTAL TIME
300 KCAL PER SERVING
SUITABLE FOR
VEGETARIANS

900g/2lb floury
   potatoes
1 onion
2tbls finely chopped
   fresh parsley
salt and freshly ground
   black pepper
50g/2oz butter
vegetable oil, for greasing

1 Scrub the potatoes and cook them in their skins in boiling, lightly salted water for 15–20 minutes or until they are barely tender. Meanwhile, finely chop the onion.

2 Remove the pan from the heat, drain the potatoes in a colander and cool them under cold running water. When the potatoes are cool enough to handle, strip off the skins with a sharp knife.

3 Grate the skinned potatoes into a large bowl, using the coarsest blade of the grater. Then mix in the chopped onion, parsley, salt and pepper.

4 Heat the butter in a heavy-based frying pan about 23cm/9in in diameter. When the fat is quite hot, add the potato mixture and pat it lightly into a large flat, round cake with a spatula or fish slice. Cook the rösti over a low heat for 10–15 minutes or until the underside is crusty and browned.

5 Grease a plate with oil. Using a spatula, turn the rösti on to the plate and slide it back in the frying pan. Fry gently for a further 10–15 minutes or until the underside is crisp and well-browned. Turn the rösti out on to a warm serving dish, cut into wedges and serve at once.

SERVING SUGGESTIONS

Swiss Potato Rösti is a great way to use up leftover potatoes. Simply store the potatoes in the fridge in an airtight container and use within 24 hours. For a filling breakfast dish, try adding some crispy strips of bacon to the grated potato before you fry the cake.

WHAT TO DRINK

This tasty potato dish is great washed down with a young Rioja, a fresh and juicy red wine from Spain.

ROAST POTATO CHIPS

THE SIMPLICITY OF THESE DELICIOUS GARLIC ROASTED POTATO CHIPS MEANS THAT YOU WILL WANT TO MAKE THEM AGAIN AND AGAIN

SERVES 4–6
15 MINS TO PREPARE
1 HR TOTAL TIME
252 KCAL PER SERVING
SUITABLE FOR VEGETARIANS

2tbls olive oil
3 garlic cloves, crushed
900g/2lbs potatoes
2tbls fresh thyme leaves, stripped off the stems
salt and freshly ground black pepper

1 Heat the oven to 425°F/ 220°C/gas 7. Put the oil and garlic in a large, shallow roasting tin and heat in the oven for 5 minutes.

2 Scrub the potatoes, then cut them into 1.5cm/¹/2in-square chips. Pat the chips dry with kitchen towels.

3 Take the roasting tin out of the oven and put over low heat on top of the hob. Toss the potatoes and thyme in the hot oil until well coated.

4 Return the roasting tin to the oven and roast the potatoes for about 40 minutes until they are golden brown. Remove the roasting tin from the oven and season the potatoes with salt and freshly ground black pepper to taste.

INGREDIENTS GUIDE

This recipe works equally well with new potatoes or main-crop potatoes. If the potatoes are very old you may prefer to peel them, rather than just scrubbing them, but the dish has extra flavour if you leave the skins on.

NUTRITION NOTES

Tuck into these crunchy roast potato chips as a healthier alternative to the traditional deep-fat fried chips or sauté potatoes.

SERVING SUGGESTIONS

Serve these garlicky potato chips with grilled chops and steaks, omelettes or roast meats.

WHAT TO DRINK

Match these delicious roast potato chips with a glass of chilled Beaujolais — the pungent flavours of onion and garlic would suggest a red rather than a white.

SPICY POTATO & PEA BHAJI

IN THIS INDIAN VEGETABLE DISH, POTATOES
AND PEAS ARE GIVEN A REAL LIFT BY ADDING A
HOT GREEN CHILLI AND CURRY SPICES
SERVES 4 · 20 MINS TO PREPARE
55 MINS TOTAL TIME · 255 KCAL PER SERVING
SUITABLE FOR VEGETARIANS

1 green chilli
3–4tbls vegetable oil
1 onion, thinly sliced
1tsp ground turmeric
1tsp cumin seeds
1/4tsp ground ginger
450g/1lb potatoes, peeled and diced
225g/1/2lb frozen peas
2tbls chopped fresh coriander

1 Heat the oven to 180°C/350°F/gas 4. Wearing rubber gloves, slit the chilli in half lengthways. Use a teaspoon to scoop out the seeds and discard them. Finely chop the chilli, removing and discarding the white membrane; set the chilli aside.

2 Heat the oil in a frying pan and fry the onion over medium heat for 5–7 minutes or until browned but not crisp, stirring frequently. Over low heat, stir in the turmeric, cumin seeds, ginger, chilli and potatoes and cook for 5 minutes, stirring frequently.

3 Transfer the onion and potato mixture to a casserole, add the frozen peas and stir well. Cover and bake for 15–20 minutes or until the potatoes are tender. To serve, turn the bhaji into a serving dish, garnish with the chopped coriander and serve hot.

INGREDIENTS GUIDE
As a general rule, red chillies tend to be 'sweeter' than green ones, and the darker a green chilli is, the hotter it will be. Thin, pointed chillies tend to be hotter than short, rounded ones. However, despite these guidelines, there are exceptions and some chillies can be surprisingly hot. When preparing them, bear in mind that the tip of the chilli is the mildest part and the seeds are the hottest.

1 Sift the flour and a generous pinch of salt into a bowl. Make a well in the centre. Pour in the lightly beaten egg and a little of the milk. Using a wooden spoon, beat the mixture, gradually incorporating the milk to make a smooth batter. When smooth, beat in the remaining milk and the melted butter. Cover and leave the batter to stand for at least 30 minutes.

2 Meanwhile, thinly peel the potatoes. Using the large holes on a grater, grate the peeled potatoes coarsely on to 2 or 3 layers of kitchen towels. Pat them dry firmly with a tea towel to extract as much of the excess liquid they contain as possible.

3 Stir the grated potatoes into the prepared batter and season generously with freshly ground black pepper.

CRÊPES PARMENTIER

ANTOINE-AUGUST PARMENTIER POPULARIZED THE POTATO IN FRANCE AND HIS NAME ON A RECIPE INDICATES THAT IT CONTAINS POTATO
SERVES 4 · 45 MINS TO PREPARE
1 1/4 HRS TOTAL TIME WITH RESTING · 260 KCAL PER SERVING
SUITABLE FOR VEGETARIANS

50g/2oz flour
salt and freshly ground black pepper
1 large egg, lightly beaten
5tbls milk
1tbls melted butter
225g/8oz floury potatoes
olive oil, for greasing
25g/1oz butter

4 Grease a large heavy-based frying pan with a wad of kitchen towels dipped in olive oil. Heat the pan and add half the butter. Using 2 tablespoons of the potato batter for each crêpe, spoon 4 crêpes into the pan, well away from one another, spreading the batter in thin circles.

5 Cook the crêpes over a gentle heat for about 5 minutes, or until the undersides are golden. Turn them over with a spatula and cook for a further 5 minutes or until crisp, golden and cooked right through.

6 Transfer the cooked crêpes to a heated serving platter and keep them hot. Add the remaining butter to the pan and cook the remaining batter as above. Serve at once.

SWEET POTATO CHIPS

SERVES 4 · 15 MINS TO PREPARE
30 MINS TOTAL TIME · 535 KCAL PER SERVING
SUITABLE FOR VEGETARIANS

900g/2lb sweet potatoes
salt
oil for deep frying
finely chopped fresh parsley, to garnish (optional)

1 Scrub the sweet potatoes. Bring a saucepan of salted water to the boil, add the sweet potatoes and cook for 10 minutes or until just tender.

2 Drain them well and cut into chips, about 5cm/2in long and 5mm/¼in wide. Drain the chips once more on 2 or 3 layers of kitchen towels.

3 Heat the oil in a deep-fat frier or deep pan to 190°C/375°F. At this temperature a 15mm/½in cube of day-old bread will turn golden in 50 seconds. Fry the chips a small quantity at a time for 3 minutes, or until crisp and golden with a soft floury centre.

4 As each batch is cooked, drain well and spread on 2 or 3 layers of kitchen towels to absorb the excess oil, while frying the next batch in the same way and at the same temperature.

5 Sprinkle the chips with salt, and a little finely chopped parsley, if wished, and serve as quickly as possible while they are still hot.

OATY FRIED POTATOES

THIS IS A DELICIOUS WAY TO SERVE POTATOES
WITH GRILLED HERRING OR MACKEREL
SERVES 4 · 5 MINS TO PREPARE · 35 MINS TOTAL TIME
280 KCAL PER SERVING · SUITABLE FOR VEGETARIANS

450g/1lb small new potatoes
salt
1 large egg, beaten
3tbls porridge oats
50g/2oz butter
1 bunch watercress, divided into sprigs, to garnish

1 Bring a large pan of salted water to the boil, add the potatoes and cook for about 15 minutes until just tender. Drain well and leave to cool slightly.

2 Put the beaten egg on a plate and dip the potatoes in it, to coat thoroughly, shaking off any excess. Put the porridge oats on a plate. Coat a few potatoes at a time in the oats so that they are well covered, pressing the oats on with your fingers to make them stick firmly.

3 Melt the butter in a frying pan until it is just beginning to sizzle, then add the oat-covered potatoes. Fry them over moderate heat, turning frequently, for about 5 minutes until they are an even golden brown.

4 Transfer the potatoes to a warmed serving dish and tuck in watercress sprigs at regular intervals between the potatoes. Serve at once.

SWEET POTATO PIE

SERVES 4–6 · 15 MINS TO PREPARE · 1¼ HRS TOTAL TIME
380 KCAL PER SERVING · SUITABLE FOR VEGETARIANS

450g/1lb fresh or tinned
   sweet potatoes, peeled
   and finely grated
1 egg, beaten
50g/2oz butter, melted
75ml/2fl oz milk
50g/2oz plain flour
375g/13oz tin crushed

pineapple
25g/1oz fresh white
   breadcrumbs
15g/¹/2oz butter, for
   topping
extra butter, for
   greasing

1   Heat the oven to 170°C/325°F/gas 3. In a large bowl
thoroughly combine all the ingredients except for the
breadcrumbs and the 15g/¹/2oz butter.

2   Pour the mixture into a well-greased 1.1L/2pt dish
and bake for 40 minutes until light golden, or 20 minutes if using tinned potatoes.

3   Mix the breadcrumbs well with the butter. Sprinkle
the top of pie with this mixture and return to the
oven for another 15 minutes until the pie is quite firm and
the topping brown.

VARIATIONS

Instead of topping with breadcrumbs, cover the top of the pie
with 75g/3oz marshmallows, which will melt and brown. Americans
serve this with turkey and cranberry sauce at Thanksgiving. Try
mixing 1 teaspoon of ground cinnamon with the topping.

SPICY YELLOW POTATOES

SERVES 4 · 30 MINS TO PREPARE · 1 HR TOTAL TIME
340 KCAL PER SERVING · SUITABLE FOR VEGETARIANS

900g/2lb potatoes
salt
225g/8oz frozen peas
2tbls vegetable oil
1 onion, finely chopped
1 garlic clove, crushed
   (optional)
2tsp whole black mustard

seeds, crushed
1tsp ground turmeric
1tsp very finely grated
   fresh root ginger
25g/1oz butter
2tbls milk
coriander leaves, to
   garnish

1   Bring the potatoes to the boil in a large saucepan of
salted water, lower the heat and simmer for 20 minutes until tender. Meanwhile, cook the peas according to
packet instructions.

2   Heat the oil in a frying pan, add the onion and garlic,
if using, and fry gently until the onion is soft and lightly coloured. Add the crushed mustard seeds, turmeric and
ginger and cook for 1 minute, stirring.

3   Drain the potatoes thoroughly and mash with the
butter and milk. Drain the peas. Stir the onion mixture into the mashed potatoes and beat well to mix. Stir in
the drained peas and season with salt to taste.

4   Turn the potatoes into a warmed serving dish, garnish
with coriander leaves and serve at once.

CRUNCHY CURRIED POTATOES

SERVE THESE SPICY POTATOES WITH PLAINLY
COOKED MEAT TO
MAKE A MORE EXOTIC MEAL
SERVES 4 · 30 MINS TO PREPARE
1 HR 10 MINS TOTAL TIME · 255 KCAL PER SERVING
SUITABLE FOR VEGETARIANS

700g/1 1/2lb potatoes cut into large chunks
salt
2tbls vegetable oil
25g/1oz margarine or butter
1tbls mild curry powder
freshly ground black pepper
juice of 1/2 lemon
margarine, for greasing

1 Heat the oven to 200°C/400°F/gas 6. Lightly grease an ovenproof dish. Put the potatoes in a pan of salted water, bring to the boil, then reduce the heat and simmer for about 15 minutes until almost tender. Drain the potatoes and arrange them in a single layer in the greased dish.

2 Heat the oil and margarine in a small saucepan. Add the curry powder and cook for 1 minute over moderate heat, stirring with a wooden spoon. Pour this mixture over the potatoes, turning them to make sure they are all coated. Season with salt and pepper to taste and turn again.

3 Bake the potatoes in the oven for 25 minutes, then turn them and bake for a further 15 minutes, until they are tender and crunchy. Sprinkle them with the lemon juice and serve at once.

SOUPS & LIGHT SUPPERS

USE POTATOES TO MAKE THICK, WHOLESOME SOUPS PERFECT FOR BOTH WINTER AND SUMMER MENUS, AS WELL AS A RANGE OF POPULAR SNACKS AND LIGHT SUPPER DISHES.

CREAM OF POTATO SOUP

THIS FILLING SOUP MAKES A DELICIOUS LUNCH
OR SUPPER DISH SERVED WITH SLICES OF
HOT FRENCH BREAD
SERVES 4 · 20 MINS TO PREPARE
1 HR TOTAL TIME · 305 KCAL PER SERVING
SUITABLE FOR VEGETARIANS

450g/1lb floury potatoes, diced
50g/2oz butter
2 large onions, finely chopped
450ml/³/4pt milk
450ml/³/4pt vegetable or chicken stock
salt and freshly ground black pepper
4tbls single cream
chopped chives or parsley, to garnish

1 Melt the butter in a pan and, when the foam has sub-
sided, add the potatoes and onions. Cook gently for
about 5 minutes until the vegetables are soft. Stir
frequently to prevent any of the vegetables from sticking to
the bottom of the pan.

2 Add the milk and stock, season with salt and pepper
to taste and bring to the boil. Lower the heat and
simmer for 30 minutes, stirring occasionally, until the potatoes are tender.

3 Allow the mixture to cool a little, then work through
a sieve or work until smooth in a blender or food
processor.

4 Return the soup to the rinsed-out pan and reheat.
Taste and adjust the seasoning if necessary. Stir in the
cream just before serving. Pour into a large tureen, or ladle
into individual soup bowls, garnish with the chopped chives
or parsley and serve at once.

COOK'S TIPS

The flavour of this soup is vastly improved by using homemade
stock, rather than a stock cube.

WATCHPOINTS

Once the cream has been added to the soup, do not allow it to
boil, otherwise the cream will separate and spoil the appearance of
the soup.

WATERCRESS SOUP

SERVES 4 · 20 MINS TO PREPARE
40 MINS TOTAL TIME · 245 KCAL PER SERVING

2 potatoes
2 bunches or bags of watercress
1 bunch of spring onions
75g/3oz butter
900ml/1¹/2pt chicken stock
salt and pepper
4tbls single cream

1 Peel and slice the potatoes. Trim off the watercress
stalks and roughly chop the leaves, reserving a few
sprigs for the garnish. Chop the spring onions roughly.

2 Melt the butter in a deep saucepan and add the potatoes. Cook, covered, over low heat for 8 minutes. Add
the watercress and spring onions and cook for a further
5 minutes. Add the stock and simmer for 10–15 minutes
or until the potatoes are tender.

3 Allow the soup to cool slightly then work until
smooth in a blender or food processor. Return the
soup to the pan, season with salt and pepper to taste
and heat through. To serve, pour the soup into four
bowls. Add 1 tablespoon of cream to each swirling the
cream with a skewer. Garnish each bowl with watercress
sprigs and serve at once.

VICHYSSOISE

SERVES 6 · 20 MINS TO PREPARE
3¹/2 HRS TOTAL TIME WITH CHILLING
315 KCAL PER SERVING · SUITABLE FOR VEGETARIANS

50g/2oz butter
4 leeks, white part only, sliced
2 onions, chopped
2 celery sticks, chopped
3 large or 4 medium potatoes, sliced
1.1L/2pt hot vegetable stock
salt and freshly ground black pepper
pinch of grated nutmeg
pinch of cayenne pepper
450ml/³/4pt double cream, chilled
4tbls finely snipped chives

1 Melt the butter in a large saucepan. Add the leeks, onions and celery and fry over a low heat, stirring occasionally, for 10 minutes or until the vegetables are soft but not coloured. Add the potatoes and stock and simmer for 30 minutes or until the potatoes are tender.

2 Either work the soup until smooth in a blender or food processor, or work through a sieve. Season with salt and pepper, nutmeg and cayenne pepper to taste. Allow the soup to cool, then chill.

3 When ready to serve, decant the soup into a chilled soup tureen, or individual bowls, pour in the cream and sprinkle with the snipped chives.

CHEESY POTATO SOUP

SERVES 4 · 20 MINS TO PREPARE · 1 HR 10 MINS TOTAL TIME
335KCAL PER SERVING · SUITABLE FOR VEGETARIANS

700g/1¹/2lb potatoes, cut into even-sized pieces
salt
25g/1oz butter
1 large onion, chopped
2 large garlic cloves, finely chopped (optional)
3 celery sticks, chopped
1 large carrot, diced
¹/4 small swede, diced
300ml/¹/2pt vegetable or chicken stock
150ml/¹/4pt milk
¹/2tsp dried thyme
¹/2tsp celery salt
freshly ground black pepper
75g/3oz Cheddar cheese, grated
3tbls chopped parsley

1 Boil the potatoes in salted water for 15–20 minutes or until tender. When cooked, leave them to cool slightly in the water, then transfer both potatoes and water to a blender and blend until smooth or pass them through a sieve. Return the purée to the rinsed-out pan. Melt the butter in a frying pan, add the onion and garlic and fry over moderate heat until beginning to soften. Add the remaining vegetables and cook, stirring occasionally, for about 10 minutes, until beginning to colour.

2 Mix the vegetables with the potato purée and stir in the stock, milk, thyme and celery salt. Add pepper to taste. Bring to the boil, lower the heat and simmer gently for 15 minutes or until the vegetables are just soft. Stir in the cheese, reserving 2 tablespoons, and simmer for a further 2–3 minutes. Season if necessary. Sprinkle with the parsley and the remaining cheese and serve at once.

1 Heat the oil in a large, heavy-based saucepan, then add the onion and garlic and cook over medium heat for 3 minutes. Add the water, vegetable stock and potatoes. Bring to the boil, then simmer for 10 minutes or until the potatoes are soft.

2 Remove the pan from the heat and work the contents in a food processor or blender until smooth. Return the purée to the saucepan and season with salt and freshly ground black pepper to taste.

3 Add the cabbage to the saucepan. Bring the soup back to simmering point, then remove from the heat and pour into a large serving bowl.

4 Grind black pepper over the top, then ladle the soup into four individual serving bowls and serve at once with large fried bread croûtons.

CABBAGE & POTATO SOUP

THIS SIMPLE CABBAGE SOUP (KNOWN AS CALDO VERDE) IS FROM PORTUGAL. THE CABBAGE LEAVES ARE ADDED AT THE LAST MINUTE SO THAT THEY KEEP THEIR COLOUR
SERVES 4 · 15 MINS TO PREPARE · 35 MINS TOTAL TIME
265 KCAL PER SERVING · SUITABLE FOR VEGETARIANS

2tbls olive oil
1 large onion, finely chopped
2 garlic cloves, finely chopped
600ml/1pt water
600ml/1pt vegetable stock
450g/1lb potatoes, peeled and sliced
salt and freshly ground black pepper
350g/12oz cabbage leaves, finely shredded
large fried bread croûtons, to serve

WHAT TO DRINK
This flavoursome, traditional soup from Portugal tastes even more delicious when accompanied by a crisp white Vinho Verde from the northern region of the country.

NUTRITION NOTES
This tasty soup is a meal in itself, and is particularly useful for those on low fat or vegetarian diets because both cabbage and potatoes contain significant amounts of essential fibre and vitamin C.

VARIATIONS
For a more robust soup, use ham or chicken stock instead of vegetable stock, and divide 50g/2oz sliced chorizo sausage between the individual servings.

ALOO KA SHORVA (POTATO SOUP)

SERVES 6 · 15 MINS TO PREPARE · 1 HR TOTAL TIME
270 KCAL PER SERVING · SUITABLE FOR VEGETARIANS

1 onion
2 garlic cloves
4 potatoes
2tbls vegetable oil
1tsp curry powder
salt
600ml/1pt water or vegetable stock
225ml/8fl oz milk
1tsp dried mint leaves
1 extra potato, grated and deep fried, for garnish

1 Finely chop the onion and garlic. Peel the potatoes and cut into small cubes. Heat the oil in a heavy-based saucepan and fry the onion and garlic until softened. Add the potatoes, curry powder, salt and water or stock. Bring to the boil, then reduce the heat and simmer for 20 minutes or until the potatoes are cooked.

2 Add the milk and mint and simmer for 5 minutes longer. Then remove from the heat, cool slightly and work to a purée in a blender. Reheat the soup before serving. Sprinkle with the fried grated potato and serve very hot.

SMOKED FISH CHOWDER

SERVES 4 · 25 MINS TO PREPARE
55 MINS TOTAL TIME · 350 KCAL PER SERVING

50g/2oz butter
1 onion, sliced
1 leek, finely sliced
1/2 red pepper, finely sliced
2 potatoes, diced
450g/1lb smoked haddock
    or cod, skinned and cut
into large chunks
1 bay leaf
300ml/1/2pt milk
200g/7oz tin sweetcorn,
    drained
2tbls chopped fresh
    parsley

1 Melt the butter in a large saucepan over medium heat. Add the onion, leek and pepper and fry for 3 minutes or until slightly softened, stirring often. Add the potatoes and stir well to coat with butter. Reduce the heat to low, cover the pan and cook for 5 minutes, stirring often.

2 Add the fish, bay leaf, milk and 275ml/1/2pt water. Increase the heat to medium and bring to the boil, then replace the lid and lower the heat. Simmer gently for 15 minutes or until the fish is cooked and the potatoes are tender, stirring occasionally.

3 Add the sweetcorn to the chowder and simmer for 2–3 minutes to heat through. Remove the bay leaf and serve hot, sprinkled with the chopped parsley.

WHAT TO DRINK
A New Zealand Sauvignon Blanc, with its herby notes and hint of gooseberry, would go well with this rich soup.

CRUNCHY POTATO SKINS

THESE CRISPY COOKED POTATO SKINS ARE AN AMERICAN IDEA – SERVE THEM EITHER AS A SNACK ON THEIR OWN, OR BEFORE A MAIN COURSE OF THICK, JUICY BURGERS AND SALAD

SERVES 4
30 MINS TO PREPARE
2 HRS TOTAL TIME
330 KCAL PER SERVING
SUITABLE FOR VEGETARIANS

4 large potatoes, scrubbed
225ml/8fl oz sour cream
1tbls snipped chives
salt and freshly ground black pepper
vegetable oil, for deep frying
4tbls mayonnaise
4tbls finely snipped chives

1 Heat the oven to 200°C/400°F/gas 6. Prick the potatoes all over with a fork, then bake in the oven for 1–1 1/2 hours or until they are tender when gently squeezed.

2 Meanwhile, mix the sour cream and chives together with salt and pepper to taste. Spoon into a serving bowl and refrigerate.

3 When the potatoes are tender, remove them from the oven and leave to cool slightly. Cut each one in half lengthways, scoop out the cooked potato and discard (see Cook's Tips). Cut the skins in half again.

4 Heat the oil in a deep-fat frier with a basket to 190°C/375°F, or until a day-old bread cube browns in 50 seconds. Place the potato skins in the basket. Lower the basket into the oil and deep-fry for 2–3 minutes until they are brown and crispy.

5 Take the basket out of the oil, shake it, then lift the cooked potato skins on to kitchen towels. Drain, then put them on to a serving plate. Sprinkle with plenty of salt and place 1 tablespoon of mayonnaise and 1 tablespoon of snipped chives on top of each. Serve at once.

COOK'S TIPS
Don't waste all the left-over cooked potato flesh: mash it with plenty of butter and use as a topping for pies.

POTATO WEDGES WITH TARRAGON DIP

SERVE THESE
DELICIOUSLY CRUNCHY CHUNKS OF SPICY
BAKED POTATO WITH THEIR ACCOMPANYING
TARRAGON DIP AS A STARTER, SNACK OR
BUFFET-PARTY VEGETABLE DISH
SERVES 4 · 10 MINS TO PREPARE · 30 MINS TOTAL TIME
305 KCAL PER SERVING · SUITABLE FOR VEGETARIANS

4 medium-sized baking
potatoes
3tbls corn oil
1tbls barbecue seasoning

DIP
150ml/¹/4pt fromage frais
juice of half a lemon
3tbls chopped tarragon
sprig of fresh tarragon,
to garnish

1 Heat the oven to 200°C/400°F/gas 6. Scrub the potatoes and cut them in half lengthways, then cut each

WHAT TO DRINK

The delicious combination of spicy baked potato wedges with a fresh, tarragon dip is excellent with a lightly chilled bottle of Californian Chardonnay.

half into three or four wedges. Put the oil and barbecue seasoning in a bowl, then dip the potato wedges in the mixture and drain slightly on kitchen towels.

2 Put the potato wedges on a wire rack in a baking tray and bake for about 20 minutes or until the wedges are well browned and crunchy.

3 Meanwhile, prepare the dip. Combine all the ingredients in a food processor or blender for 30 seconds, or beat them together in a bowl. Put the dip in a small bowl with the potato wedges around it. Garnish with a sprig of fresh tarragon.

VARIATIONS

If you want to spice up the tarragon dip a little, add some cayenne pepper, or a crushed clove of garlic. You could also add pieces of well grilled bacon for those who like meat, or make two dips for a buffet-style party.

NUTRITION NOTES

Baked potatoes are a healthy, low-fat food, provided you don't smother them with too much butter. In this recipe all the fibre and vitamin C is retained because they are baked in their skins.

POTATO RAMEKINS

SERVES 4 · 15 MINS TO PREPARE · 35 MINS TOTAL TIME
300 KCAL PER SERVING · SUITABLE FOR VEGETARIANS

450g/1lb potatoes, peeled
salt and freshly ground black pepper
1tbls milk
75g/3oz butter
1tsp chopped fresh parsley
1/2tsp chopped fresh basil
50g/2oz fresh Parmesan cheese, grated
25g/1oz fresh white breadcrumbs

1 Bring the potatoes to boil in salted water, lower the heat and cook for 20 minutes. Drain and mash with the milk and 50g/2oz butter. Beat until smooth, then season to taste. Heat the grill to high.

2 Stir the parsley, basil and cheese into the potato mixture and spoon into ramekin dishes. Do not allow the potato mixture to get cold.

3 Divide the breadcrumbs between the dishes and dot with the rest of the butter. Place under the grill for 3 minutes until the tops are golden. Serve at once.

COOK'S TIPS

Ready-grated Parmesan, easily available packaged from supermarkets, may be used instead of fresh cheese. Alternatively, use a strong Cheddar.

CHEESE & POTATO SCONES

MAKES 8–10 SCONES · 15 MINS TO PREPARE
30 MINS TOTAL TIME · 125 KCAL PER SCONE
SUITABLE FOR VEGETARIANS

100g/4oz mature Cheddar
cheese, grated
100g/4oz self-raising flour
2tsp baking powder
1/4tsp salt
good pinch of mustard
powder

25g/1oz butter, diced
100g/4oz potatoes,
boiled, mashed and
cooled
1 small egg
1tbls milk
vegetable oil, for greasing

1 Heat the oven to 190°C/375°F/gas 5. Grease a baking sheet. Sift the flour, baking powder, salt and mustard into a bowl. Rub in the butter until the mixture resembles breadcrumbs, then stir in the cheese until thoroughly mixed.

2 Sieve the potatoes into the flour mixture and mix together with a round-bladed knife. Beat the egg with the milk, then pour slowly into the flour and potato mixture, adding just enough liquid to mix to a soft dough.

3 Turn the dough out on to a well-floured surface and knead lightly. Roll out the dough to a thickness of 2cm/3/4in and cut into circles with a 5cm/2in cutter. Knead the remaining dough and roll out again to cut more circles. Put the scones on to the prepared baking sheet and bake for about 15 minutes, until golden brown. Cool for a few minutes on a wire tray, then serve warm.

1 Use a heavy-based frying pan with a lid for this recipe. Heat the oil over medium heat and fry the onions for 3 minutes, stirring occasionally. Reduce the heat to low and add the potato. Cover and cook for 15–20 minutes or until the potato and onion are soft, stirring occasionally.

2 Stir in the chorizo and cook for 2–3 minutes or until the sausage is heated through. Meanwhile, beat the eggs together with the salt, pepper and parsley.

3 Pour the eggs into the pan over the potato and sausage mixture. Cover and leave to cook over a low heat for about 30 minutes or until the eggs are set.

4 Invert the tortilla on to a warmed serving plate and cut into quarters to serve, garnished with chopped parsley.

TORTILLA WITH CHORIZO SAUSAGE

SERVE THIS SUBSTANTIAL EGG AND POTATO DISH WITH A SALAD OF SLICED PEPPERS AND ACCOMPANY WITH CRUSTY BREAD

SERVES 4 · 10 MINS TO PREPARE
1 HR 10 MINS TOTAL TIME
585 KCAL PER SERVING

4tbls olive oil
2 onions, sliced
450g/1lb potatoes, cubed
**175g/6oz chorizo sausage,
  cut into 12mm/1/2in cubes**
6 eggs
salt and freshly ground black pepper
**2tbls finely chopped fresh parsley,
  plus extra to garnish**

COOK'S TIPS
A tortilla is a kind of Spanish omelette, made with diced potato and other vegetables. Unlike a French omelette, it is cooked slowly until the eggs are set throughout, and served cut into quarters or wedges.

WHAT TO DRINK
Try a fruity, but not too oaky, red from Spain, such as new-style Rioja, a Navarra or a Penedés.

INGREDIENTS GUIDE
Chorizo is a spicy Spanish sausage made from pork highly coloured with paprika. There are two kinds, one that needs cooking and one that's ready to eat. Use the ready-to-eat kind for this dish, or use salami as a substitute.

PAPRIKA POTATOES

CARAWAY SEEDS GIVE THIS DISH A DISTINCTIVE
ANISEED TASTE WHICH IMPARTS A VERY
DEFINITE FLAVOUR TO THE MEAL
SERVES 4 · 15 MINS TO PREPARE
1 HR TOTAL TIME · 265 KCAL PER SERVING

700g/1¹/2lb potatoes
salt
2tbls vegetable oil
1 medium onion, sliced
1tsp sweet paprika, plus
   extra to garnish
300ml/¹/2pt chicken stock

¹/2tsp caraway seeds
   (optional)
1 large tomato, skinned
   and chopped
freshly ground black
   pepper
3tbls sour cream

1 Boil the potatoes in salted water for about 7 minutes or until they are beginning to soften. Drain and cut them into 5mm/¹/4in slices.

2 Heat the oil in a large saucepan and fry the onion over medium heat for about 4 minutes, or until it is just beginning to turn light brown. Add the paprika, chicken stock, caraway seeds, if using, tomato and pepper. Stir well and add the potatoes, stirring carefully.

3 Bring slowly to the boil, cover the pan and simmer for 20–25 minutes. The potatoes should have absorbed most of the liquid.

4 Pour over the sour cream and allow just to heat through. Turn out into a warmed serving dish. Sprinkle with a little extra paprika to garnish.

POTATO & CARROT LAYER

SERVES 6 · 20 MINS TO PREPARE · 1 HR TOTAL TIME
350 KCAL PER SERVING · SUITABLE FOR VEGETARIANS

1.4kg/3lb potatoes	chopped
25g/1oz butter	1tbls lemon juice
a little milk	1tbls water
salt and freshly ground	50g/2oz sultanas
black pepper	1 small piece of stem
1 onion, chopped	ginger, with 1tbls
700g/1¹/2lb carrots, diced	syrup reserved
50g/2oz shelled walnuts,	

1 Heat the oven to 190°C/375°F/gas 5. Grease a large ovenproof dish. Cook the potatoes in salted boiling water for about 15 minutes or until tender, drain, then mash them with the milk and half the butter. Season with salt and pepper to taste.

2 Meanwhile, fry the onion gently in the remaining butter until soft. Stir in the carrots, walnuts, lemon juice, water and sultanas. Simmer gently for 10 minutes until the carrots are just tender. Add the ginger and syrup. Season with salt and pepper and remove from the heat.

3 Spread one-third of the potatoes in the dish and top with half the carrots. Repeat these layers again and finish with the remaining potato. Bake in the oven for 15–20 minutes. Serve at once.

NUTTY POTATO LAYER

SERVES 4 · 35 MINS TO PREPARE · 1 HR 10 MINS TOTAL TIME
405 KCAL PER SERVING · SUITABLE FOR VEGETARIANS

900g/2lb potatoes, cut into 2cm/³/4in cubes	pinch of grated nutmeg
salt	freshly ground white pepper
25g/1oz margarine or butter	75g/3oz Cheddar cheese, grated
2 onions, cut into 5mm/¹/4in slices	50g/2oz salted peanuts, roughly chopped
3tbls milk	1tbls chopped parsley

1 Heat the oven to 200°C/400°F/gas 6. Put the potatoes in a pan of salted water, bring to the boil, then reduce the heat and simmer for about 15 minutes until tender. Meanwhile, melt the margarine in a saucepan and fry the onions gently for 5 minutes or until soft and lightly coloured. Drain on kitchen towels.

2 Drain the potatoes well and mash. Beat in the milk and nutmeg thoroughly then season with salt and pepper to taste. Spread one-third of the creamed potato over the base of a 1.25L/2pt ovenproof dish. Cover with half the onions and half the cheese. Repeat these layers again and top with the remaining potato. Decorate the surface with a fork.

3 Sprinkle the peanuts over the potato and bake in the oven for 30–35 minutes until the top turns a golden colour. Sprinkle the chopped parsley in the centre of the dish and serve at once.

JANSSON'S TEMPTATION

ONCE YOU TASTE THIS FABULOUS DISH YOU
WILL SEE WHY JANSSON WAS TEMPTED BY IT!
SERVES 6 · 20 MINS TO PREPARE
1¼ HRS TOTAL TIME
330 KCAL PER SERVING

50g/2oz tin anchovies
a little milk
75g/3oz butter
2 onions, thinly sliced into rings
700g/1½lb potatoes, very thinly sliced
300ml/½pt single cream
salt and freshly ground black pepper
flat-leaved parsley, to garnish

1 Heat the oven to 180°C/350°F/gas 4. Drain the anchovies fillets and place in a small bowl. Cover with milk. Leave to soak for 30 minutes, then drain and chop. In a frying pan, melt 25g/1oz butter and fry the onions over medium heat for 5 minutes or until they are soft, stirring frequently.

2 Grease a 1.7L/3pt ovenproof dish with 25g/1oz of the butter and place a layer of potatoes in the bottom, using up about a third of them. Add half the onions and then half of the anchovies. Make another layer of potatoes, then onions, then anchovies and finish with a layer of potatoes.

3 Dot the top layer with the remaining butter, pour over the cream and season with salt and pepper to taste. (You'll probably need very little salt, as the anchovies are salty.) Bake for 50 minutes or until the potatoes are tender and the top is golden. Garnish with a sprig or two of flat-leaved parsley and serve hot.

WHAT TO DRINK
Verdicchio, a dry white wine from Italy, has a freshness that balances the texture and taste of this potato dish.

INGREDIENTS GUIDE
If you can find Scandinavian anchovies for this dish, use them. As they are less salty than the Portuguese ones more commonly available, they do not need to be soaked in milk.

SERVING SUGGESTIONS
This creamy potato pie makes a tasty treat with some salad. It is also an ideal dish for smorgasbord, or as an accompaniment to plainly cooked meat or poultry.

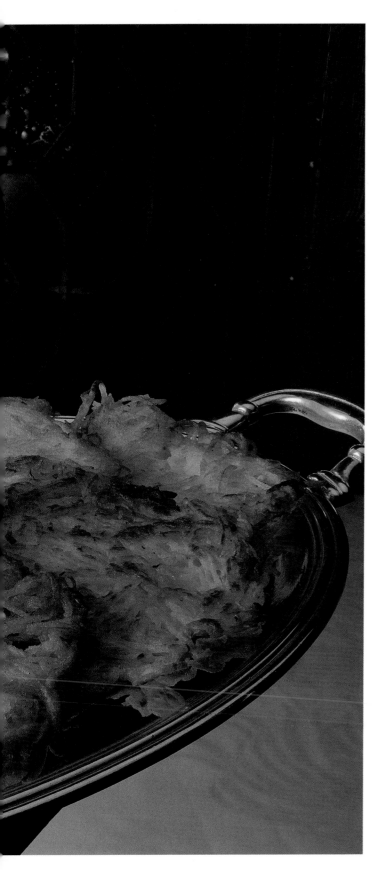

LATKES

LATKES ARE JEWISH POTATO PANCAKES. THEY
ARE PARTICULARLY GOOD WITH SALT BEEF, BUT
CAN BE SERVED WITH A SAUCE OR SAVOURY
BUTTER AS A DISH ON THEIR OWN
SERVES 6 · 15 MINS TO PREPARE
1½ HRS TOTAL TIME WITH SOAKING
375 KCAL PER SERVING · SUITABLE FOR VEGETARIANS

6 medium-sized, floury potatoes
1 onion, very finely chopped
2 medium-sized eggs, lightly beaten
2tbls plain flour
salt and freshly ground black pepper
25g/1oz butter
2tbls vegetable oil

1 Peel, then coarsely grate the potatoes. Cover with cold water and leave to soak for 1 hour. Drain, then place in a clean, dry cotton tea towel and wring out over a bowl to extract as much moisture as possible. Reserve the potato liquid.

2 Turn the potatoes into a mixing bowl and add the onion, eggs, flour and seasonings to taste. Beat together with a wooden spoon until evenly blended. If the mixture is too stiff, beat in enough of the reserved liquid to give a soft dropping consistency.

3 Heat half the butter and oil in a heavy-based frying pan. When the foam subsides, drop in the potato batter, a tablespoon at a time. Space well apart and spread out with the back of a fish slice or broad spatula.

4 Fry for about 3 minutes on each side, or until crisp and golden, turning once only. Add more butter and oil to the pan as needed. Remove the cooked latkes from the pan with a slotted spoon, drain and serve at once.

SERVING SUGGESTIONS
Made without the onion and pepper, the pancakes can be served with a dollop of thick apple sauce, with jam and sour cream, or simply sprinkled with sugar and cinnamon — delicious for breakfast.

COOK'S TIPS
Save the remaining potato liquid as stock for soups.
Always fry latkes in batches, taking care not to overcrowd the pan. Although best served straight from the pan, you can keep the cooked pancakes hot in a warm oven while you fry the remainder.

CHEESY POTATO CAKE

SERVES 4
40 MINS TO PREPARE
1 HR 40 MINS TOTAL TIME WITH CHILLING
320 KCAL PER SERVING
SUITABLE FOR VEGETARIANS

700g/1½lb potatoes, peeled
25g/1oz butter
1 large onion, finely chopped
1 garlic clove, crushed
salt and freshly ground black pepper
pinch of grated nutmeg
2tbls chopped fresh parsley
75g/3oz Cheddar cheese, grated
flour for dusting
3tbls home-made breadcrumbs
1 egg, beaten

1 Cut the potatoes into even-sized pieces, put them in a saucepan of boiling water and simmer for 20 minutes or until tender. Drain and mash with a fork, then leave to cool.

2 Melt the butter in a saucepan over low heat. Add the onion and fry over low heat for 10 minutes or until soft. Add the garlic and cook for a further 2 minutes.

3 Add the cold mashed potato to the onion and garlic mixture and season with salt and pepper to taste. Stir in the nutmeg, parsley and 50g/2oz of the grated cheese.

4 Turn the mixture out on to a lightly floured work surface and form into an 18cm/7in round with a thickness of about 20mm/¾in. Slide on to a greased baking sheet.

5 Mix the remaining cheese and the breadcrumbs together on a plate. Brush the top and sides of the potato cake with beaten egg, then scatter over the breadcrumb mixture. Score the top into four wedges. Chill in the fridge for 20 minutes.

6 Heat the oven to 200°C/400°F/gas 6. Put the baking sheet in the oven and cook the potato cake for 25 minutes until golden brown. Cut into wedges to serve.

SERVING SUGGESTIONS
Serve this delicious cheesy potato cake hot with a spicy tomato sauce and fresh mixed salad

VARIATIONS
If you prefer, use six finely chopped spring onions instead of the large onion. For extra colour and flavour, use 350g/12oz potatoes and 350g/12oz carrots.

HAM & POTATO CAKES

SERVES 4 · 25 MINS TO PREPARE
45 MINS TOTAL TIME · 385 KCAL PER SERVING

450g/1lb potatoes, grated	25g/1oz butter
1 large onion, grated	50g/2oz fresh white
100g/4oz sliced cooked	breadcrumbs
ham, chopped	1tbls finely chopped
salt and freshly ground	fresh parsley
black pepper	25g/1oz Cheddar cheese,
50g/2oz lard or dripping	grated

1 Mix together the grated potatoes and onion and put them into a colander or large sieve. Press down with a plate and squeeze out all the surplus liquid. Put the potato and onion mixture into a bowl. Mix in half the chopped ham and season well with salt and pepper. Divide the mixture into four portions and shape each portion into a round about 10cm/4in in diameter.

2 Heat the lard in a large frying pan. Add the ham and potato cakes and fry over medium heat for 8–10 minutes on each side or until golden and cooked through. Meanwhile, melt the butter in a separate small saucepan or frying pan. Stir in the breadcrumbs and cook for about 10 minutes over low heat until the breadcrumbs are crisp and golden, stirring frequently.

3 Stir the remaining chopped ham into the fried bread-crumbs with the parsley and grated cheese, and spoon the breadcrumb mixture equally over the top of each potato cake. Serve at once.

HERBY POTATO CAKE

SERVES 6 · 30 MINS TO PREPARE · 2½ HRS TOTAL TIME
WITH SOAKING · 255 KCAL PER SERVING
SUITABLE FOR VEGETARIANS

700g/1½lb potatoes	1tsp bicarbonate of soda
50g/2oz butter	salt and freshly ground
1 large onion, thinly sliced	black pepper
1 garlic clove, finely	2tbls chopped parsley
chopped (optional)	1tsp dried thyme
100g/4oz plain white or	1 large egg, beaten
wholemeal flour	butter, for greasing

1 Grate the potatoes into a large bowl of water and leave them to soak for 1 hour. Heat the oven to 180°C/350°F/gas 4.

2 Melt half of the butter in a frying pan. Add the onion and garlic, if using, and fry gently for about 10 minutes or until soft but not coloured. Stir in the remaining butter until melted, then remove from the heat.

3 Sift the flour with the bicarbonate of soda on to a plate and season well with salt and pepper. Drain the soaked potatoes in a colander, pressing down hard to remove as much water as possible. Put the potatoes into a bowl. Mix in the flour and herbs, then the onion mixture and finally the egg.

4 Press the mixture into a greased 25cm/10in flan tin and bake in the oven for 1 hour or until the top is brown. Serve at once.

SPICED POTATO CAKES

SERVES 4 · 30 MINS TO PREPARE · 2¼ HRS TOTAL TIME
325 KCAL PER SERVING · SUITABLE FOR VEGETARIANS

3 large hot baked potatoes
1 tsp salt
1 tsp spice blend
1 large egg
2tbls each finely chopped
  red and green peppers
ghee or vegetable oil
1 tsp coriander seeds

ghee or vegetable oil
2 tomatoes, skinned,
  seeded and chopped
150ml/¼pt double cream
½tsp ground turmeric
chilli powder
salt and freshly ground
  black pepper

SAUCE
¼ onion, finely chopped
1 garlic clove, chopped
3 thin slices fresh ginger
1–2tsp spice blend

SPICE BLEND
1 tsp cardamom seeds
½tsp cumin seeds
¼tsp whole cloves
2tsp coriander seeds

1 Remove the flesh from the potatoes, reserving 225g/8oz. Mash the potato with the salt, spice blend and egg. Mix well. Blanch the pepper for 1 minute in boiling water, drain, refresh and add to the potato mixture.

2 Make the sauce: sauté the onion, garlic, ginger and 1 teaspoon spice blend in 1 teaspoon ghee until the onion is translucent. Add the tomatoes, cream and turmeric, and season with chilli powder and salt and pepper. Simmer gently for 2–3 minutes. Meanwhile, form 8 potato cakes from the mashed potato and fry them in ghee until crisp. Serve sprinkled with coriander seeds on top of the sauce on a warmed serving dish.

HASH BROWNS

SERVES 4–6 · 20 MINS TO PREPARE · 1 HR 50 MINS TOTAL TIME
315 KCAL PER SERVING · SUITABLE FOR VEGETARIANS

1.2kg/2½lb large floury potatoes
1 large onion, chopped
salt and freshly ground black pepper
25g/1oz butter
2tbls olive oil
1tbls finely snipped chives

1 Heat the oven to 200°C/400°F/gas 6. Scrub the potatoes and put them on a baking tray. Bake for 1 hour or until soft when gently squeezed.

2 Holding the potatoes in a tea towel, remove the skins with a sharp knife and put the flesh into a bowl. Add the onion and mash with a fork until free of lumps. Season with salt and freshly ground black pepper to taste.

3 Heat the butter and oil in a heavy-based frying pan. When the foaming subsides, add the potato mixture. Flatten it into a cake with a palette knife. Cook over a low heat for 30 minutes, shaking the pan occasionally and lifting the edges to make sure the mixture is not burning or sticking to the frying pan. The underside should be crusty and well browned.

4 Turn the potato cake out on to a round, heated serving dish, slightly larger than the frying pan. Serve as soon as possible, sprinkled with chives.

POTATO & SPINACH CROQUETTES

FOR AN UNUSUAL ALTERNATIVE TO CHIPS, TRY THESE TASTY CROQUETTES MADE FROM A MIXTURE OF TWO EVERYDAY VEGETABLES
SERVES 4–6 · 35 MINS TO PREPARE
1 HR TOTAL TIME · 340 KCAL PER SERVING
SUITABLE FOR VEGETARIANS

450g/1lb potatoes, peeled and cut into large, even-sized pieces
450g/1lb spinach
1 egg yolk, lightly beaten
2tbls grated mature Cheddar cheese
3tbls flour, plus extra for dusting
salt and freshly ground black pepper
2 eggs
75g/3oz dry white breadcrumbs
vegetable oil for deep-frying

1 Put the potatoes in a large pan, cover with water and bring to the boil, then reduce the heat and simmer for 15 minutes or until the potatoes are tender. Drain them thoroughly, then rub through a sieve to purée.

2 Meanwhile, wash the spinach well and remove and discard any large stalks. Place the spinach, still wet, in a large saucepan. Cover and cook over low heat for 5 minutes or until tender, stirring once or twice, then drain very thoroughly and chop the spinach finely.

3 Put the potato purée and spinach in a large bowl, beat in the egg yolk and cheese and season to taste. On a floured surface, roll the potato mixture into fat sausage shapes about 5cm/2in long.

4 Put the flour on a plate and season with salt and pepper to taste. Beat the eggs lightly in a shallow bowl and put the breadcrumbs on a separate plate.

5 Roll each croquette in the flour, the egg and then the breadcrumbs, making sure they are evenly coated with each ingredient.

6 Heat the oil in a deep fat fryer to 180°C/350°F. The oil is hot enough when a 12mm/1/2in square of day-old white bread turns golden brown in 1 minute. Deep fry the croquettes, in batches, for 2 minutes or until they are golden brown. Drain on kitchen towels and serve hot.

WHAT TO DRINK
A fresh dry white wine, such as a Galestro from Tuscany, would go well with this vegetable dish.

brown. Remove from the heat and set aside to cool for about 15 minutes. Meanwhile, season the potatoes with salt and pepper to taste. Spread the flour and breadcrumbs out on separate large flat plates. Beat the egg in a shallow bowl.

2 Spread about 2 tablespoons of potato evenly over each sausage and mould it over the sausage with your fingers. Roll each sausage lightly in flour then flatten gently between the palms of the hands. Dip the sausages in beaten egg, then roll in the toasted breadcrumbs until they are evenly coated.

4 Heat the oven to 110°C/225°F/gas¹/4. Pour enough oil into a deep-fat frier with a basket to cover the croquettes. Heat the oil to 190°C/375°F, or until a day-old bread cube browns in 50 seconds.

5 Lower 4 croquettes into the oil and deep fry for 5 minutes until golden brown. Drain on kitchen towels and keep warm in the oven while frying the remaining sausage croquettes. Serve at once.

SAUSAGE CROQUETTES

SERVE THESE CROQUETTES WITH A SALAD OF
CUCUMBER, TOMATO AND ONION RINGS
SERVES 4 · 40 MINS TO PREPARE
1¹/4 HRS TOTAL TIME · 560 KCAL PER SERVING

450g/1lb potatoes
salt
450g/1lb pork sausages
freshly ground black pepper
25g/1oz plain flour
100g/4oz toasted breadcrumbs
1 large egg
vegetable oil, for deep-frying

Boil the potatoes in salted water for 15 minutes or until tender. Drain well, mash and allow to cool. Heat the grill to medium. Prick the sausages well with a fork and grill for 10–15 minutes, turning frequently until golden

SERVING SUGGESTIONS

Allow 2 croquettes per person for a supper dish or 1 per person for a snack.

INGREDIENTS GUIDE

Choose large sausages: there should be 8 sausages in a 500g/1lb packet. There is now a wide variety of flavoured sausages available in most supermarkets. Try using Lincolnshire, farmhouse or tomato-flavoured sausages for extra taste.

WATERCRESS & POTATO CROQUETTES

SERVE AS AN INTERESTING ACCOMPANIMENT TO PLAINLY COOKED MEAT OR AS A LIGHT VEGETARIAN SNACK WITH A SALAD
SERVES 4–6 · 40 MINS TO PREPARE
1 HR 55 MINS TOTAL TIME WITH COOLING AND CHILLING
410 KCAL PER SERVING · SUITABLE FOR VEGETARIANS

700g/1 1/2lb potatoes
salt
25g/1oz margarine or butter
2tbls milk
freshly grated nutmeg
freshly ground black pepper
1 bunch watercress, finely chopped
2 eggs, beaten
flour for dusting
50g/2oz blanched almonds, finely chopped
4tbls fresh white breadcrumbs
150ml/1/4pt vegetable oil

TO GARNISH
watercress sprigs
lime twists (optional)

1 Bring the potatoes to the boil in salted water, lower the heat and cook for 20 minutes. Drain the potatoes and mash with the margarine and milk until smooth. Season with nutmeg, salt and pepper to taste, then beat in the watercress and about one-quarter of the beaten eggs. Leave the mixture for about 30 minutes to cool.

2 Dust a work surface with flour. Divide the mixture into 12 portions and, with floured hands, roll each into cork shapes.

3 Mix the almonds with the breadcrumbs and spread out on a large flat plate. Dip the croquettes first in the remaining beaten egg, then roll in the almond and breadcrumb mixture. Refrigerate for at least 30 minutes.

4 Heat the oven to 110°C/225°F/gas 1/4. Heat the oil in a large heavy-based frying pan to 190°C/375°F or until a day-old bread cube browns in 50 seconds when immersed.

5 Fry a batch of the croquettes in the hot oil for about 5 minutes, until golden brown and crisp, then remove with a slotted spoon and drain on kitchen towels. Keep warm in the oven while frying the rest of the croquettes. Garnish with watercress and lime twists, if liked, and serve.

FREEZING
Drain and cool the fried croquettes. Open freeze until solid, then pack in rigid containers, separating layers with foil. Seal, label and return to freezer for up to 3 months. To serve: defrost in a single layer on a baking sheet at room temperature for 2 hours, then cover and reheat in a 180°C/350°F/gas 4 oven for 20 minutes.

COOK'S TIPS
Chilling firms up the mixture, which helps to prevent the croquettes from breaking up during frying. However, chilling is not absolutely necessary — if you are short of time just take extra care when frying the croquettes to ensure that they don't disintegrate.

NEW POTATOES WITH WINE

A DELICIOUSLY DIFFERENT WAY OF COOKING
NEW POTATOES, THIS DISH CAN BE
SERVED AS A LIGHT MEAL WITH CRISPY
GRILLED BACON
OR TOPPED WITH POACHED EGGS
SERVES 4 · 15 MINS TO PREPARE
1 HR TOTAL TIME · 220 KCAL PER SERVING

700g/1 1/2lb new potatoes, scrubbed
25g/1oz butter
1/2 small tin anchovies, drained,
   soaked in milk for 20 minutes,
   then drained and chopped
1tbls finely chopped fresh mint, chives or parsley
salt and freshly ground black pepper
150ml/1/4pt dry white wine
1tbls finely grated Parmesan cheese

1 Heat the oven to 190°C/375°F/gas 5 and grease a shallow ovenproof dish with half of the butter. Bring the potatoes to the boil in salted water, lower the heat and cook for 12–15 minutes or until barely tender. Drain and leave until cool enough to handle.

2 Slice the potatoes into the prepared dish, sprinkling each layer with the anchovies, mint, chives or parsley and salt and pepper to taste. Pour the wine over the top, then sprinkle evenly with Parmesan cheese before finally dotting the potatoes with the remaining butter.

3 Bake the dish towards the top of the oven for about 30 minutes or until the potatoes are cooked through and the top is crisp and golden brown. Serve at once, straight from the dish.

SERVING SUGGESTIONS

New potatoes with wine can also be served as an unusual and tasty vegetable accompaniment to roast meat and poultry. Because this dish includes anchovies, it is also suitable for serving with a main course of fish.

COOK'S TIPS

Cook the potatoes in this style when the oven is already in use for other dishes, for example, when roasting meat or poultry. Anchovies are salty, so only a very light seasoning of salt is necessary.

POTATO-STUFFED PANCAKES

THIS IS A TASTY AND SUBSTANTIAL INDIAN
PANCAKE, OR DOSA, WHICH ALSO MAKES A
LOVELY BRUNCH DISH
SERVES 6 · 1 HR TO PREPARE
1½ DAYS TOTAL TIME WITH SOAKING AND COOLING
405 KCAL PER SERVING
SUITABLE FOR VEGETARIANS

FILLING
4 potatoes, peeled
3 onions
1 green chilli
2.5cm/1in piece fresh
  root ginger
2tbls oil or melted ghee
½tsp mustard seeds
½tsp turmeric powder
a few curry leaves
salt to taste

PANCAKES
100g/4oz split black
  beans or grams
250g/½lb rice flour
1tsp baking powder
salt to taste
300–450ml/½–¾pt
  water
225ml/8fl oz oil for frying

1 To make the pancakes, wash the black beans or grams thoroughly, then cover them with cold water and leave to soak overnight. The next day, drain the beans and grind to a paste with the flour in a food processor. Put the paste into a large bowl, cover and leave in a cool place for at least 8 hours. Add the baking powder and salt, with sufficient water to make a thick batter.

2 Heat 1 tablespoon of oil in a heavy-based frying pan. When smoking, pour a large spoonful of the batter into the centre and, with a wooden spoon, gently spread the batter in a circular movement until it is 10–15cm/ 4–6in in diameter. Cook the pancake for 2–3 minutes, on one side only. Lift the pancakes out of the pan very carefully so as not to break them and put them on to a clean tea towel. Repeat the cooking process until all the batter is used, adding more oil to the pan as necessary.

3 To make the filling: boil the potatoes with two of the onions until tender. Drain, then mash the potatoes and slice the onions. Finely slice the remaining onion, the green chilli and the root ginger. Heat the oil or ghee in a heavy-based pan and add the mustard seeds. As soon as they 'pop', add the sliced raw onion, the chilli, root ginger, turmeric and curry leaves. Cook the mixture, stirring, until the onion is golden brown.

4 Next add the mashed potatoes and sliced boiled onions and stir to mix well. Add salt to taste. Cook for a further 1–2 minutes, stirring continuously, then remove the mixture from the heat.

5 Place a spoonful of the potato filling into the centre of each dosa and fold the pancake over the filling. Serve at once, or heat a little more oil or ghee in the frying pan and cook the filled dosas quickly on both sides to crisp them.

ITALIAN-STYLE WAFFLES

SERVES 4 · 15 MINS TO PREPARE · 50 MINS TOTAL TIME
WITH SOAKING · 415 KCAL PER SERVING

50g/2oz tin anchovies
a little milk
25g/1oz margarine or
butter
1 large onion, finely
chopped
1 garlic clove, crushed
(optional)
8 thin streaky bacon
rashers

8 frozen potato waffles
1tbls capers
1tbls vinegar drained
from capers
2tbls tomato purée
1tbls finely chopped
fresh parsley
2tbls water
freshly ground black
pepper

1 Drain the anchovies and soak them in milk for 20 minutes. Drain again then chop. Melt the margarine in a saucepan, add the onion and garlic, if using, and fry gently for 10 minutes. Meanwhile, heat the grill to high. Grill the bacon until crisp, then grill the potato waffles according to the packet instructions and keep hot.

2 Add the anchovies, capers, vinegar, tomato purée, parsley and water to the onion in the pan. Mix well together and continue cooking for 2–3 minutes, stirring. Season with pepper to taste.

3 Transfer the waffles to a warmed serving dish. Top each waffle with a spoonful of the prepared sauce. Crumble the bacon rashers and sprinkle over the top of the waffles. Serve at once.

POTATO & PEPPER PANCAKES

SERVES 4 · 10 MINS TO PREPARE · 25 MINS TOTAL TIME
290 KCAL PER SERVING · SUITABLE FOR VEGETARIANS

450g/1lb potatoes
50g/2oz green pepper,
deseeded and finely
chopped
1 onion, finely chopped
4tbls plain flour

1 large egg
4tbls milk
salt and freshly ground
black pepper
25g/1oz margarine
5tbls vegetable oil

1 Heat the oven to 110°C/225°F/gas 1/4. Coarsely grate the potatoes into a colander and press down with a plate to squeeze out all the surplus liquid. Pat dry with kitchen towels and turn into a bowl. Stir in the green pepper, onion and flour. Beat the egg with the milk, season with salt and pepper to taste, then add to the potato mixture. Mix well.

2 Heat the margarine and half the oil in a large heavy-based frying pan over medium heat. When sizzling, drop in tablespoons of the potato mixture, flattening each mound into a pancake shape with a fish slice.

3 Fry the pancakes for about 4 minutes on each side until golden brown. Remove from the pan with a slotted spoon and drain on kitchen towels. Keep hot in the oven while frying the remaining mixture in the same way, adding more oil with each batch. Arrange the pancakes on a warmed serving dish and serve at once.

1 Layer the aubergine cubes in a colander, sprinkling each layer with salt. Put a plate on top and weight down. Leave to drain for about 30 minutes to remove the bitter juices from the aubergine. Rinse the cubes under cold running water, pat them dry with kitchen towels or a clean tea towel and set aside.

2 Heat the oil in a large frying pan, add the aubergine cubes, beef stock, tomato purée, crushed garlic, if using, and sugar. Season with salt and pepper to taste.

3 Bring the mixture to the boil, then lower the heat, cover the pan and simmer for 8–10 minutes, stirring frequently, until the liquid is absorbed and the aubergine is tender.

4 Meanwhile, heat the grill to high and toast the waffles for 4 minutes on each side taking care not to burn them, or fry as directed on the packet.

5 Place the waffles in a flameproof dish, pile the aubergine mixture on top and sprinkle over the grated cheese. Grill for 1–2 minutes or until the cheese starts to bubble. Garnish the waffles with coriander sprigs or parsley and serve at once.

AUBERGINES ON WAFFLES

IF YOU LIKE THE TASTE OF AUBERGINES, TRY THEM ON POTATO WAFFLES FOR AN ORIGINAL SNACK OR LIGHT MEAL
SERVES 4 · 30 MINS TO PREPARE
1 HR 20 MINS TOTAL TIME WITH DRAINING
295 KCAL PER SERVING

2 large aubergines, cut into cubes
salt
2tbls vegetable oil
300ml/¹/2pt beef stock
4tsp tomato purée
2 garlic cloves, crushed (optional)
¹/2tsp dark soft brown sugar
freshly ground black pepper
4 potato waffles
75g/3oz Cheddar cheese, grated
coriander sprigs or parsley, to garnish

SERVING SUGGESTIONS

This dish makes a light lunch or snack; for a more substantial meal double the quantities and serve 2 waffles per person.

COOK'S TIPS

The cheese can be sprinkled on top of the aubergines and allowed to melt just before serving without grilling if preferred.

POTATO GNOCCHI WITH BROCCOLI

IN SOME PARTS OF ITALY,
POTATO GNOCCHI
(TINY DUMPLINGS)
ARE SERVED AS AN
ALTERNATIVE TO PASTA.
HERE THEY ARE COMBINED
WITH CHOPPED BROCCOLI
FOR A TASTY LIGHT MEAL
SERVES 4–6
40 MINS TO PREPARE
1 HR 10 MINS TOTAL TIME
588 KCAL PER SERVING
SUITABLE FOR VEGETARIANS

**700g/1½lb potatoes, peeled
and cut into chunks
1 egg, beaten
50g/2oz plain flour, sifted
50g/2oz freshly grated
Parmesan cheese
salt and freshly ground
black pepper
ground nutmeg
flour for dusting
225g/8oz small broccoli florets
50g/2oz butter
150ml/¼pt single cream**

1 Put the potatoes in a steamer and cook them for about 20 minutes or until tender. When cooked, put them on kitchen towels to dry off a little, then rub them through a sieve into a large mixing bowl.

2 Add the egg, the flour and 25g/1oz of the Parmesan cheese and beat well to blend. Add salt, freshly ground black pepper and a little ground nutmeg to taste.

3 Liberally dust your hands and the work surface with flour, then put some of the potato mixture on the work surface and form into a long sausage shape with a diameter of roughly 25mm/1in. Cut the sausage into pieces about 25mm/1in long, then flatten them slightly using the back of a fork. Repeat with the remaining mixture.

4 Either steam the broccoli florets or cook in boiling water until they are just tender, then put them in an ovenproof serving dish with the butter dotted over and keep warm in a low oven.

5 Bring a large saucepan of water to a gentle simmer, then drop the gnocchi in, about 10 at a time. When they drop to the bottom of the pan and, after a few seconds, rise to the top, remove them immediately using a slotted spoon and put them in the ovenproof dish with the broccoli florets. Keep warm while you cook the remaining gnocchi.

6 When all the gnocchi are cooked, drizzle the cream over the top and stir very gently, without breaking up the gnocchi. Sprinkle with the remaining Parmesan cheese, then put the dish under a hot grill for about 5 minutes or until the cheese is just beginning to brown. Serve the dish at once, lightly sprinkled with more freshly ground black pepper to taste.

POTATO GNOCCHI & TOMATO SAUCE

SERVES 4 · 1¼ HRS TO PREPARE · 1¾ HRS TOTAL TIME
380 KCAL PER SERVING · SUITABLE FOR VEGETARIANS

TOMATO SAUCE
1 small onion, finely
  chopped
1 garlic clove, crushed
  (optional)
150g/5oz tin tomato
  purée
300ml/½pt water
1 tsp sugar
1 bay leaf
pinch of dried basil
salt and freshly ground
  black pepper

GNOCCHI
700g/1½lb potatoes
100g/4oz plain flour
25g/1oz butter, softened
pinch of freshly grated
  nutmeg
1 egg yolk, beaten
50g/2oz Parmesan
  cheese, grated
margarine or butter for
  greasing

1 Make the sauce first: place all the ingredients in a pan with salt and pepper to taste. Bring to the boil, then reduce the heat, cover and simmer gently for 30 minutes. Meanwhile, bring the potatoes to the boil in salted water, reduce the heat and cook for 20 minutes until tender. Drain, then rub through a sieve into a bowl.

2 Work the sauce through a sieve, then return to the rinsed-out pan. Set aside. Grease an ovenproof dish and heat oven to 110°C/225°F/gas ¼.

3 Beat the flour into the potatoes with the butter, nutmeg and salt and pepper to taste. Add just enough of the beaten egg yolk to bind the mixture. Work in 40g/1½oz of the grated Parmesan.

4 Bring a large pan of lightly salted water to a simmer. Meanwhile, turn the potato mixture on to a floured surface, divide into three portions and form each piece into a roll about 2.5cm/1in in diameter. Cut each roll into 2.5cm/1in slices. Drop slices from one roll into the simmering water. Cook for about 5 minutes, or until they rise to the surface and look puffy. Remove with a slotted spoon, place in the prepared dish and keep hot in the oven while you cook the remaining pieces in the same way.

5 Reheat the tomato sauce. Heat the grill to high. Pour a little of the warmed tomato sauce over the gnocchi and top with the remaining Parmesan. Grill for about 5 minutes until the top is bubbling. Serve at once, with the remaining sauce handed separately in a warmed jug.

BAKED POTATOES

WITH A LITTLE IMAGINATION AND A FEW READILY-AVAILABLE, INEXPENSIVE INGREDIENTS, IT IS EASY TO TURN THE HUMBLE BAKED POTATO INTO AN EXCITING, ALL-IN-ONE FEAST

BAKED POTATOES WITH HADDOCK

SERVES 4 · 20 MINS TO PREPARE
1 HR 55 MINS TOTAL TIME · 720 KCAL PER SERVING

**4 large potatoes, each
  about 250g/9oz
450g/1lb smoked haddock
  fillets
600ml/1pt milk
4 black peppercorns**

**75g/3oz butter
1tbls plain flour
100g/4oz Cheddar
  cheese, grated
salt and freshly ground
  black pepper**

1 Heat the oven to 200°C/400°F/gas 6. Scrub the potatoes and prick each potato on both sides with a fork. Bake in the oven for 11/4 hours or until they feel soft when gently squeezed.

2 Meanwhile, make the filling: put the fish in a shallow frying pan and add the milk and peppercorns. Bring to the boil, reduce the heat, and simmer for 10 minutes, until the fish flakes easily. Lift the fillets carefully from the milk. Strain the milk and reserve. Cut the fish into large pieces, discarding the skin and any bones. Put the fish into a bowl.

3 Melt 25g/1oz butter in a saucepan, sprinkle in the flour and stir over low heat for 1–2 minutes until straw coloured. Remove the saucepan from the heat and gradually stir in the reserved milk. Return to the heat and simmer, stirring, until thick and smooth. Pour half the sauce over the fish and mix in well. Stir the grated cheese into the remaining sauce.

4 Remove the potatoes from the oven (leaving the oven on). Cool slightly, then cut in half lengthways. Scoop the cooked potato into a bowl reserving the shells. Add 25g/1oz butter and the cheese sauce to the potato and mash well. Season. Spoon the fish mixture into the potato shells and the mashed potato on top. Grease an ovenproof dish, place the shells in it and return to the oven for 10 minutes. Served topped with the remaining butter.

BAKED POTATO WITH WARM SPINACH SALAD

SERVES 4 · 20 MINS TO PREPARE
11/4 HRS TOTAL TIME · 565 KCAL PER SERVING

**4 potatoes
1 large red pepper
4tbls olive oil
1 small red onion, sliced
  into rings
100g/4oz pancetta, cut
  into small chunks
2tsp white wine vinegar
1tsp pesto**

**175g/6oz baby spinach
  leaves, washed and
  thoroughly dried
100g/4oz Gruyère
  cheese, cubed
freshly ground black
  pepper
4 knobs of butter**

1 Heat the oven to 200°C/400°F/gas 6. Scrub the potatoes, prick with a fork and bake for 11/4 hours or until soft. Meanwhile, core and deseed the pepper while whole. Bake for 15 minutes, turning once after 7 minutes. Remove the pepper from the oven and slice into rings while still hot holding with a clean tea towel.

2 To make the dressing, heat a little olive oil in a frying pan over medium heat. Add the onion and pancetta and cook until crisp. Turn off the heat and stir in the remaining olive oil, the wine vinegar and the pesto.

3 Put the spinach, cheese cubes and pepper into a bowl. Reheat the dressing until it starts to bubble, then pour it over the salad. Sprinkle with freshly ground black pepper, then toss all the ingredients together until they are well mixed. Cut the potatoes open and place a knob of butter in each. Serve at once with the salad.

CRISPY TUNA JACKETS

IN THIS RECIPE THE JACKETS ARE MADE EXTRA
CRISPY BY RUBBING THEM WITH OLIVE OIL
BEFORE COOKING

SERVES 4
10 MINS TO PREPARE
1 HR 40 MINS TOTAL TIME
530 KCAL PER SERVING

4 large baking potatoes
olive oil
25g/1oz butter
200g/7oz tin tuna in brine, drained
2 celery sticks, halved lengthways and finely chopped
4tbls snipped fresh chives
175g/6oz Cheddar cheese, finely grated
salt and freshly ground
black pepper

1 Heat the oven to 190°C/375°F/gas 5 and place a baking sheet inside. Scrub the potatoes well and pat them dry. Prick them all over with a fork, then use your hands to rub olive oil all over the skins.

2 Put the potatoes on the baking sheet and bake for 1–1¼ hours or until the jackets are very crisp and the potatoes feel soft when you squeeze them gently.

3 Remove the potatoes from the oven and set aside until they are cool enough to handle. Meanwhile, heat the grill. Cut a slice off the top of each potato and scoop all the flesh out into a bowl using a spoon. Take care not to pierce the skins. Set the skins aside. Add the butter to the bowl, then lightly mash with a fork. Stir in the tuna, celery, chives and 100g/4oz of the cheese. Beat together.

4 Divide the filling roughly into 4 portions. Spoon a portion into each potato skin, pressing it down so that the skins are well filled, and piling it into a mound on top. Sprinkle the remaining cheese over each potato, put them in a grill pan and grill for about 2 minutes or until the cheese melts and turns golden brown. Serve at once.

INGREDIENTS GUIDE

The best potatoes for baking are main crop ones that contain the most starch, so that the flesh becomes fluffy during cooking. Apart from King Edwards, other suitable varieties include Cara, Maris Piper and Pentland Squire.

MICROWAVE MAGIC

Potatoes microwave well, but the skins won't become as crispy as they do when rubbed with olive oil and baked in a conventional oven. To microwave, prick each potato several times, and arrange in a circle on a double thickness of kitchen towel on the floor of the microwave. Cook on High (100 per cent) for about 20 minutes, turning the potatoes once after 10 minutes, until they are tender.

BAKED POTATOES WITH SAUSAGE & BEANS

SERVES 4 · 10 MINS TO PREPARE
1 HR 40 MINS TOTAL TIME · 540 KCAL PER SERVING

4 baking potatoes
4 sausages
100g/4oz button mushrooms, halved
400g/14oz tinned baked beans in tomato sauce
dash of Worcestershire sauce
50g/2oz Cheddar cheese, grated
vegetable oil for frying

1 Heat the oven to 200°C/400°F/gas 6. Scrub the potatoes and prick them on both sides with a fork. Bake them on a rack in the oven for 1¼ hours.

2 Twenty minutes before the potatoes are ready, start frying the sausages according to the instructions on the packet. Add the mushrooms to the frying pan 5 minutes before the sausages are done, stirring occasionally to ensure that they cook evenly. Meanwhile, heat the beans slowly in a saucepan until warmed through and stir in the Worcestershire sauce.

3 When cooked, halve the potatoes and fill with the baked beans. Cut the sausages into bite-size pieces and pile with the mushrooms on top of the beans. Sprinkle with the cheese and place under a hot grill for 5 minutes or until the cheese has melted. Serve at once.

CHEESE-BAKED POTATOES

SERVES 6 · 15 MINS TO PREPARE
3½ HRS TOTAL TIME WITH COOLING · 445 KCAL PER SERVING
SUITABLE FOR VEGETARIANS

6 medium-sized baking potatoes
4tbls single cream
50g/2oz butter, softened
37–50g/1½–2oz Parmesan cheese, freshly grated
salt and freshly ground black pepper

1 Heat the oven to 200°C/400°F/gas 6. Scrub the potatoes and prick them on both sides with a fork. Bake them on a rack in the oven for 1¼ hours. Allow to cool. Reduce the oven temperature to 190°C/375°F/gas 5.

2 With a sharp, serrated-edged knife, cut a shallow, horizontal slice from each potato and discard. Using a small spoon, carefully scoop out the cooked potato pulp into a large mixing bowl. Take care not to break the skins and try to leave the shell about 6mm/¼in thick.

3 Add the cream, butter and cheese to the potato pulp, together with the salt and freshly ground black pepper to taste. Mash the ingredients together until thoroughly blended, then divide the mixture among the six shells. Add an extra sprinkling of cheese on top of the potato if you wish. Place the stuffed potatoes on a baking tray and bake for 25–30 minutes, or until heated through.

VARIATIONS

For a perfect vegetarian meal, omit the bacon rolls and add tomato slices on top of the cheese in step 3.

COOK'S TIPS

To make bacon rolls, roll four trimmed rashers of streaky bacon. Grill the bacon rolls in an ovenproof dish for 10 minutes, or until crispy.

CHEESE SOUFFLÉ POTATOES

SERVES 4 · 15 MINS TO PREPARE · 1¾ HRS TOTAL TIME
565 KCAL PER SERVING

4 medium-sized baking potatoes
50g/2oz butter
175g/6oz mature Cheddar cheese, grated and extra for sprinkling (optional)
½tsp mustard powder
salt and freshly ground black pepper
2 large eggs, separated
bacon rolls and chives, to garnish (optional)

Heat the oven to 200°C/400°F/gas 6. Scrub the potatoes and prick them all over with a fork. Bake them on a rack in the oven for 1¼ hours or until soft when gently squeezed. Remove the potatoes from the oven.

2 Reduce the temperature of the oven to 190°C/375°F/ gas 5. Cut each potato in half lengthways. Scoop out the flesh, leaving a 6mm/¼in shell. Mash the flesh until smooth, then mix in the butter, cheese, mustard powder, egg yolks and salt and pepper to taste. Whisk the egg whites until stiff and fold into the potatoes. Fill the potato shells with the mixture.

3 Put the potatoes back into the oven and bake for 8–10 minutes, or until the filling is just set. If wished, add an extra sprinkling of cheese to the top of the potatoes and cook for a further 5 minutes, or until the cheese starts to melt and turn golden brown. Garnish with the bacon rolls and chives, if wished, and serve at once.

SURPRISE POTATOES

SERVES 4 · 45 MINS TO PREPARE · 1³/4 HRS TOTAL TIME
500 KCAL PER SERVING · SUITABLE FOR VEGETARIANS

4 large potatoes, unpeeled
150g/5oz cottage cheese
150g/5oz Cheddar cheese, grated
2 spring onions, finely chopped
2 gherkins, finely chopped
salt and freshly ground black pepper
50g/2oz butter
margarine, for greasing

1 Heat the oven to 180°C/350°F/gas 4 and grease an ovenproof dish with margarine. Bring the potatoes to the boil in salted water, lower the heat and cook for 20 minutes or until tender.

2 Meanwhile, make the filling: put the cottage cheese in a bowl, together with the Cheddar cheese, onions, gherkins and salt and pepper to taste. Mix well.

3 Drain the cooked potatoes, cool, and cut in half lengthways. Using a teaspoon, carefully scrape out a hollow in each half to a depth of about 2.5cm/1in, leaving a thick shell so that the potatoes will retain their shape.

4 Place 4 potato halves, hollow side upwards, in the ovenproof dish. Spoon in the filling, piling it up high. Place the other potato halves on top of the filled halves, to enclose the filling. Top each potato with a knob of butter, cover the dish and bake in the oven for 1 hour until the potatoes are cooked through. Serve at once.

EGG 'N' BACON POTATOES

SERVES 4 · 15 MINS TO PREPARE · 1³/4 HRS TOTAL TIME
455 KCAL PER SERVING

4 large baking potatoes
100g/4oz streaky bacon
100g/4oz Cheddar cheese
15g/¹/2oz butter
4tbls milk
2 eggs, separated
3tbls chopped fresh parsley
salt and freshly ground black pepper

1 Heat the oven to 200°C/400°F/gas 6. Scrub the potatoes and prick them on both sides with a fork. Bake them on a rack in the oven for 1¹/4 hours. Grill the bacon until crisp and chop it. Grate the cheese finely.

2 Take the potatoes from the oven, cut them in half lengthways and scoop out the centres. Mash the scooped-out potato with the butter, milk and egg yolks. Mix in the bacon, cheese, parsley and salt and pepper to taste. Whisk the egg whites until stiff and fold them gently into the mixture.

3 Pile the mixture back into the potato shells. Put the potato halves on to an ovenproof plate and put them back into the oven for 15 minutes or until the filling rises and becomes golden brown.

CHUNKY CHILLI JACKETS

SERVES 4 · 10 MINS TO PREPARE
1 HR 40 MINS TOTAL TIME · 445 KCAL PER SERVING

4 baking potatoes	beans, drained
2tbls oil	1/4tsp mild chilli powder
1/2lb minced steak	1/4tsp ground turmeric
1 onion, chopped	2tsp tomato purée
215g/7oz tin chopped	salt and freshly ground
tomatoes	black pepper
215g/7oz tin red kidney	50g/2oz butter

1 Heat the oven to 200°C/400°F/gas 6. Scrub the potatoes and prick them on both sides with a fork. Bake them on a rack in the oven for 1 1/4 hours.

2 Meanwhile make the chilli: heat the oil in a deep frying pan and fry the onion for 10 minutes stirring occasionally. Add the minced steak and keep stirring until evenly browned. Next add the tomatoes and kidney beans and mix thoroughly. Stir in the chilli powder, turm-eric, tomato purée and salt and pepper to taste. Increase the heat until it is simmering, then reduce the heat and continue to cook it slowly until the potatoes are tender.

3 Cut the lid from the top of each potato. Scoop out some of the flesh and mash it with a fork, adding the butter. Refill each potato with the mash, adding the chilli to the hollow on top. Serve at once.

NEAPOLITAN POTATOES

SERVES 4 · 15 MINS TO PREPARE · 1 1/2 HRS TOTAL TIME
285 KCAL PER SERVING · SUITABLE FOR VEGETARIANS

4 baking potatoes	1tsp chopped fresh basil
1 small onion, sliced	salt and freshly ground
1 garlic clove, crushed	black pepper
2tsp olive oil	25g/1oz butter, softened
4 tomatoes, skinned,	2tbls milk
seeded and sliced	175g/6oz mozzarella, cut
50g/2oz button mush-	into small cubes
rooms, sliced	cherry tomato slices and
2tsp tomato purée	basil sprigs, to garnish

1 Heat the oven to 200°C/400°F/gas 6 and bake the potatoes for 1 1/4 hours. Meanwhile, fry the onion and garlic in the oil for 10 minutes until softened. Add the tomatoes, mushrooms, tomato purée, basil, and salt and pepper to taste, and continue stirring occasionally for another 20 minutes until the sauce thickens. Keep warm.

2 Cut each baked potato in half lengthways and scoop out the flesh leaving a 5mm/1/4in shell. Mash the potato flesh with the butter, milk and salt and pepper to taste. Reserve 12 cubes of mozarella; stir the remaining cheese into the potato mixture. Divide the potato mixture between the shells. Spoon the tomato sauce over the potatoes and top with the reserved mozzarella. Place the potatoes under a hot grill until the cheese has started to melt and turn golden. Garnish with tomato slices and basil sprigs. Serve at once.

BAKED POTATOES WITH APPLE

SERVES 4 · 15 MINS TO PREPARE · 1¾ HRS TOTAL TIME
280 KCAL PER SERVING · SUITABLE FOR VEGETARIANS

4 large potatoes, about 250g/9oz each
½ medium cooking apple
25g/1oz margarine or butter
1 large onion, finely chopped
4 sage leaves, chopped
½tsp mustard powder
salt
margarine or butter, for greasing

1 Heat the oven to 200°C/400°F/gas 6. Scrub the potatoes and prick each one with a fork on both sides. Bake the potatoes in the oven for 1¼ hours.

2 Remove the potatoes from the oven (leaving the oven on), allow to cool slightly, then cut each one in half lengthways. Scoop the cooked potato into a bowl, leaving the shells intact. Mash the potato well. Peel, core and finely chop the apple.

3 Melt the margarine in a small frying pan, add the onion and fry gently until it begins to soften, stirring occasionally. Stir in the apple and cook for a further 2–3 minutes or until soft.

4 Stir the apple and onion mixture into the mashed potato. Add the sage, mustard and a little salt. Mix thoroughly. Spoon the mixture back into the potato shells and make criss-cross patterns on the top with a fork for a decorative finish.

5 Put the potato shells in a greased shallow ovenproof dish and return them to the oven. Bake for 15 minutes or until the tops are browned. Serve piping hot. Alternatively, top each potato with 25g/1oz of grated Cheddar cheese and grill under moderate heat until the cheese is golden brown.

CHICKEN & RICE POTATOES

SERVES 4 · 10 MINS TO PREPARE
1 HR 40 MINS TOTAL TIME · 430 KCAL PER SERVING

4 baking potatoes
50g/2oz flour
50g/2oz butter
300ml/¹/2pt milk
100g/4oz brown rice,
** cooked**
200g/8oz chicken, cooked
** and shredded**
50g/2oz tinned sweet-
** corn, drained**
8 cherry tomatoes,
** halved**
2 spring onions, sliced

1 Heat the oven to 200°C/400°F/gas 6. Scrub the potatoes and prick them on both sides with a fork. Bake them on a rack in the oven for 1¹/4 hours.

2 Twenty minutes before the potatoes are cooked, place the butter in a small saucepan over a low heat until melted. Remove the saucepan from the heat and stir in the flour. Return to the heat and cook, stirring for 1–2 minutes. Gradually blend in the milk and cook, stirring constantly, until smooth and thickened.

3 Stir the remaining ingredients into the sauce. Halve the cooked potatoes and fill with the chicken sauce. Serve at once.

COOK'S TIPS

The chicken and rice sauce can be frozen, but the tomatoes and spring onions should be left out. These are added when the sauce is reheated.

SAUCY CHICKEN JACKETS

SERVES 4 · 15 MINS TO PREPARE
2¹/4 HRS TOTAL TIME · 390 KCAL PER SERVING

1 chicken portion, about
** 350g/12oz**
4 baking potatoes
50g/2oz frozen peas
300g/11oz tin con-
** densed cream of**
** chicken soup**
¹/2tsp dried tarragon
¹/4tsp dried thyme
¹/2tsp lemon juice
salt and freshly ground
** black pepper**
25g/1oz butter
parsley sprigs, to garnish

1 Grill the chicken portion for 25 minutes, or until cooked, turning on both sides. Remove any skin and bones from the chicken and chop the flesh into small pieces. Heat the oven to 200°C/400°F/gas 6. Scrub the potatoes and prick them on both sides with a fork. Bake them on a rack in the oven for 1¹/4 hours or until tender. Meanwhile, cook the peas in boiling water for 5 minutes and drain.

2 Put the soup into a saucepan and add the chicken pieces, peas, herbs, lemon juice and salt and pepper to taste. Cook on a low heat for 15 minutes or until the sauce is heated through.

3 Cut a lid from the top of each potato and scoop out some of the flesh. Mash this with the butter and refill the potatoes. Pile the hot chicken sauce on to the potatoes and serve at once garnished with parsley sprigs.

THATCHED POTATOES

THESE POTATOES WITH THATCHED TOPS
ARE DELICIOUSLY WHOLESOME
SERVED WITH A SALAD
SERVES 4 · 20 MINS TO PREPARE
1 HR 50 MINS TOTAL TIME
270 KCAL PER SERVING
SUITABLE FOR VEGETARIANS

4 large potatoes, scrubbed
25g/1oz butter
1 onion, chopped
100g/4oz small button mushrooms, sliced
4–6tbls milk
1tsp made English mustard
2tsp snipped chives
salt and freshly ground black pepper
25g/1oz Cheddar cheese, finely grated

1 Heat the oven to 200°C/400°F/gas 6. Prick the potatoes all over with a fork, place directly on a rack in the oven and bake for 1 1/4 hours or until tender when squeezed gently in a cloth.

2 Melt the butter in a frying pan, and fry the onion gently for 5 minutes until soft. Add the mushrooms and continue cooking, stirring occasionally, for a further 5–6 minutes or until the liquid has evaporated. Transfer the onions and mushrooms to a large bowl.

3 Cut the baked potatoes in half lengthways and scoop out the cooked potato from each half. Add this to the onion mixture in the bowl, and beat together, adding sufficient milk to give

a smooth, creamy consistency. Beat in the mustard and chives and season with salt and pepper to taste.

4 Heat the grill to high. Pile the mixture back into the potato skins and run a fork over the tops to give a thatched effect. Sprinkle with the grated cheese. Place under the grill for 10 minutes or until golden brown.

VARIATIONS
Add any of the following ingredients to the potato mixture before replacing in the skins: 100g/4oz chopped boiled ham; 100g/4oz streaky bacon, fried and chopped; 175g/6oz tin tuna, drained and chopped; 2 hard-boiled eggs, chopped.

INGREDIENTS GUIDE
Choose potatoes suitable for baking. King Edward or Desirée are good choices and make sure they are even-sized so that they will take the same cooking time.

COOK'S TIPS
When fresh chives are not available, use freeze-dried chives or the green tops of spring onions snipped with scissors.

HEARTY DINNERS

FOR VEGETARIANS AND MEAT-EATERS ALIKE, THE POTATO IS THE CORE
INGREDIENT OF MANY SUBSTANTIAL AND NUTRITIOUS DISHES,
FROM PIES AND BAKES TO SOUFFLÉS AND PIZZAS, WHICH
WILL TEMPT EVERYONE TO THE TABLE.

GOLDEN FISH PIE

SERVES 4 · 20 MINS TO PREPARE
1 HR 50 MINS TOTAL TIME · 625 KCAL PER SERVING

450g/1lb firm white fish
  fillets (such as cod or
  haddock)
450g/1lb smoked fish
  fillets (such as cod or
  haddock)
475ml/17fl oz milk
2tsp fennel seeds
6 peppercorns
2 bay leaves

2 thick slices of onion
95g/3¹/2oz butter
40g/1¹/2oz flour
2tbls chopped fresh
  parsley
salt and freshly ground
  black pepper
700g/1¹/2lb potatoes,
  peeled and cut into
  even-sized pieces

1 Heat the oven to 180°C/350°F/gas 4. Skin all the fish pieces and remove any obvious bones. Put the fish in a shallow ovenproof dish with 425ml/15fl oz of the milk, the fennel seeds, peppercorns, bay leaves and onion slices. Cover, then bake in the oven for 30 minutes or until the fish flakes easily when the point of a knife is inserted into it.

2 Remove the fish from the dish using a slotted spoon and flake it into a bowl. Strain the milky liquid through a sieve into a jug to remove the bay leaves, peppercorns and onion.

3 Melt 40g/1¹/2oz of the butter in a small saucepan over low heat and add the flour. Gradually stir in the strained milky liquid and bring to the boil. Boil until the sauce thickens, stirring constantly. Stir in the chopped parsley, then pour the sauce over the flaked fish. Mix thoroughly and season with salt and black pepper to taste. Spoon the mixture into a 1.4L/2¹/2pt ovenproof dish, then set to one side.

4 Put the potatoes in a large saucepan and add enough cold water to cover them. Bring to the boil and simmer for 15 minutes or until the potatoes are tender. Strain, then add the remaining butter and milk and mash with a fork until smooth.

5 Spoon the mashed potato over the fish mixture, smooth the surface slightly with the back of a spoon, then run a fork across the surface to leave a wavy pattern on top. Increase the oven temperature to 200°C/400°F/gas 6 and bake for 30–40 minutes or until the top is golden and bubbling.

CHUNKY VEGETABLE PIE

SERVES 6 · ¹/2 HR TO PREPARE · 2 HRS TOTAL TIME
510 KCAL PER SERVING · SUITABLE FOR VEGETARIANS

25g/1oz butter
1 onion, chopped
25g/1oz flour
300ml/¹/2pt milk
2tbls wholegrain mustard
salt and pepper
2 large potatoes, cubed
225/¹/2lb swede, cubed

1 carrot, sliced
175g/6oz cauliflower
  florets
100g/4oz frozen peas
225g/¹/2lb frozen short-
  crust pastry, defrosted
1 egg, beaten
1tbls sesame seeds

1 Melt the butter and cook the onion slowly until soft. Add the flour and cook for 3 minutes, stirring constantly. Increase the heat and gradually add the milk, stirring constantly until it boils and thickens. Simmer slowly for 3–4 minutes, stirring often. Add the mustard and season to taste. Cool.

2 Heat the oven to 180°C/350°F/gas 4. Cook the potato, swede and carrot in boiling water for 5 minutes. Add the cauliflower and continue boiling until the vegetables are barely tender. Add the peas, cook for 1 minute, then drain all the vegetables and stir into the sauce. Spoon the sauce into a 1.1L/2pt ovenproof dish.

3 Roll out the pastry 4mm/¹/6in thick on a floured surface and cut a piece to cover the pie. Lay it over the dish. Glaze the pie top with beaten egg and sprinkle with sesame seeds. Press around the rim and make a small hole in the centre. Bake for 40 minutes or until golden brown. Serve hot.

ITALIAN COTTAGE PIE

SERVES 4 · 35 MINS TO PREPARE
1¼ HRS TOTAL TIME · 400 KCAL PER SERVING

225g/½lb cooked beef
25g/1oz butter
1 large onion, chopped
2 garlic cloves, chopped
225g/½lb tinned
   tomatoes
150ml/¼pt beef stock
2tsp freshly chopped basil
   or 1tsp dried oregano
salt and freshly ground

black pepper
75g/3oz button mush-
   rooms, sliced

TOPPING
450g/1lb potatoes
1 large egg
15g/½oz butter
50g/2oz grated Cheddar
   cheese

1   Mince the beef using the coarse blade of your mincer. Melt the butter in a heavy-based pan over low
heat. Sauté the onion and garlic. Stir in the beef, tomatoes,
stock, herbs, salt and pepper. Simmer for 5 minutes. Add
the mushrooms. Cover and simmer for a further 15 minutes, stirring occasionally. Turn the mince mixture into a
flameproof dish.

2   Meanwhile, peel and boil the potatoes. Drain and
mash them. Beat the egg and butter into the mashed
potatoes. Beat half the cheese into the potatoes. Pile on
top of the mince. Level the surface and mark with a fork.

3   Sprinkle the remaining cheese over the potatoes.
Brown under a hot grill for 5 minutes or until the
cheese is golden and bubbling.

FIDGETT PIE

SERVES 4 · 30 MINS TO PREPARE
1½ HRS TOTAL TIME · 530 KCAL PER SERVING

175g/6oz shortcrust
   pastry
225g/½lb potatoes
225g/½lb dessert apples
225g/½lb onions
350g/¾lb uncooked
   gammon or bacon

rashers
150ml/¼pt cold stock
salt and freshly ground
   black pepper
nutmeg
beaten egg and salt to
   glaze

1   Heat the oven to 200°C/400°F/gas 6. Roll out the
pastry to fit the top of a 850ml/1½pt pie dish. Cut off
a strip and place in position around the rim of the dish.

2   Peel and slice the potatoes thinly. Peel, core and slice
the apples. Peel and chop the onions. Cut the gammon
or bacon into 12mm/½in dice. Arrange the potatoes in the
base of the pie dish. Layer the apples, onions and bacon on
top, seasoning with salt, pepper and nutmeg. If the apples are
slightly tart, sprinkle a little sugar over them. The amount of
salt used will depend upon the saltiness of the gammon or
bacon and stock. Pour in the stock.

3   Cover with the pastry and decorate with shapes cut
out from the trimmings. Make a small hole in the top
and brush with the beaten egg to glaze. Bake for 15 minutes, then reduce the heat to 180°C/350°F/gas 4 and bake
for a further 45 minutes, covered with foil, to prevent the
pastry from getting too brown. Serve at once.

GIPSY PIE

THIS NUTRITIOUS
CHEESY VEGETARIAN
PIE IS ESPECIALLY
WARMING ON
A CHILLY
WINTER'S NIGHT
SERVES 4
35 MINS TO PREPARE
1 HR 35 MINS TOTAL TIME
405 KCAL PER SERVING
SUITABLE FOR
VEGETARIANS

**700g/1 1/2lb floury
potatoes
1 medium-sized onion
a little oil
3tbls milk
40g/1 1/2oz butter
1 medium-sized egg
175g/6oz Cheddar
cheese
6 ripe tomatoes
freshly ground black
pepper
sprigs of parsley to
garnish**

1 Heat the oven to 200°C/400°F/gas 6. Peel the potatoes, cut into chunks and cook in boiling salted water until tender. Meanwhile, peel and chop the onion and fry slowly in oil until golden.

2 Drain the potatoes and dry over low heat for 1 minute, shaking the pan occasionally, then mash them until quite smooth.

3 Put the milk and butter in a saucepan over a medium heat until the butter is melted and the milk is hot. Add the potatoes, reduce the heat to low and heat until fluffy. Remove from the heat. Beat the egg and add to the potatoes. Stir until well blended.

4 Grate the cheese and stir 150g/5oz into the potatoes. Slice the tomatoes thinly. Place one third of the potato in a deep 18cm/7in ovenproof dish and level the potato with a palette knife. Place half of the onions and a third of the tomatoes over the layer of potato. Season with freshly ground black pepper to taste.

5 Make another layer of potatoes, onions and tomatoes before adding a final layer of potato. Arrange the remaining sliced tomatoes in a pattern on top and sprinkle with the remaining cheese. Cook in the centre of the oven for 30 minutes or until golden and bubbling. Garnish with parsley and serve at once.

COOK'S TIPS

Use a deep dish to cook this pie. Do not grease it — the potato contains enough butter to prevent it from sticking. Any extra grease would make the pie fry.

VARIATIONS

For half the potato substitute either leek or spinach: if using leeks omit the onion and use 4 rashers of crisply fried crumbled bacon instead. For a slimmer's pie, use cauliflower instead of potato.

blade of a knife and then your hands. When ready, knead the dough until smooth. In a large bowl, mix together all the ingredients for the filling.

2 Divide the pastry into 6 equal portions. Roll out each piece and trim to a circle of about 23cm/9in diameter, using a plate or pan lid as a pattern. Divide the filling among the pastry circles, placing it in the middle of each one. Dampen the edges and bring up the two sides of the circle carefully to meet in the middle and enclose the filling. Seal the edges well and crimp to make a frill.

3 Arrange the pasties on well-greased baking sheets, prick the tops, brush with milk to glaze and bake for 2 hours. They can be served either hot or cold.

TIDDY OGGIES

THE NAME LITERALLY MEANS POTATO PASTIES. THE RICH SHORTCRUST PASTRY OFTEN CONTAINS DRIPPING FROM THE SUNDAY JOINT OF BEEF OR PORK WHICH MAKES IT PARTICULARLY NOURISHING

SERVES 6 · 1 HR TO PREPARE · 3 HRS TOTAL TIME · 720 KCAL PER PASTY

COOK'S TIPS
The recipe is especially useful when meat is in short supply as you can increase the ratio of vegetables to meat.

FILLING
400g/14oz beef skirt or braising steak, finely diced
1tsp freshly ground pepper
150ml/¹/4pt strong beef stock
500g/18oz potato, finely diced
250g/9oz chopped onion
200g/7oz swede, finely diced
2tsp salt

PASTRY
400g/14oz flour
1tsp salt
100g/4oz dripping
100g/4oz lard
1tbls milk

1 Heat the oven to 150°C/300°F/gas 2. Make the pastry: sift the flour and salt into a bowl and rub in the dripping and lard until the mixture resembles breadcrumbs. Add enough water – about 150ml/¹/4pt – to make a firm dough and bind together using the

HAM CHARLOTTE

THIS DISH MAKES AN EXCELLENT EVENING
MEAL SERVED WITH A GREEN VEGETABLE
OR GREEN SALAD
SERVES 4 · 20 MINS TO PREPARE
45 MINS TOTAL TIME · 465 KCAL PER SERVING

100g/¹/4lb cooked ham
75g/3oz button mush-
rooms
15g/¹/2oz butter
225g/¹/2lb cold cooked
potatoes, sliced
100g/¹/4lb fresh white
breadcrumbs
75g/3oz Cheddar cheese,
grated

CHEESE SAUCE
25g/1oz butter
25g/1oz plain flour
300ml/¹/2pt milk
40–50g/1¹/2–2oz Cheddar
cheese, grated
¹/2tsp mustard powder
salt and freshly ground
black pepper

1 Heat the oven to 200°C/400°F/gas 6. Mince the ham in a food processor or work through a mincer.

2 Make the cheese sauce: melt the butter slowly in a saucepan. Remove the pan from the heat and stir in the flour. Return to a low heat, stir gently for 1–2 minutes until smooth. Do not let it colour. Add the milk a little at a time, stirring continuously. When the mixture is smoothly blended, bring the sauce to the boil, stirring continuously. Turn the heat to low and add the cheese, mustard and seasoning. Cover the pan and simmer for 5 minutes.

3 Wipe and slice the mushrooms. Melt the butter in a separate saucepan and sauté the mushrooms lightly. Mix with the ham and then stir in the cheese sauce. Place a layer of ham and cheese mixture in the base of an ovenproof dish. Cover with the sliced potatoes.

4 Continue layering the potatoes and ham and cheese mixture in this way, ending with potatoes. Mix the breadcrumbs and grated cheese together. Sprinkle over the top. Cook in the centre of the oven for 20 minutes or until the top is golden and bubbling.

MIROTON OF BEEF

SERVES 4 · 50 MINS TO PREPARE
1 HR 40 MINS TOTAL TIME · 480 KCAL PER SERVING

350g/^{3}/4lb sliced beef or lamb	wine
2 large onions	salt and freshly ground black pepper
25g/1oz beef dripping	1 garlic clove
1tsp plain flour	1 bay leaf
300ml/^{1}/2pt beef stock	5 cold boiled potatoes
150ml/^{1}/4pt dry red	2tbls dried breadcrumbs

1 Trim any fat from the beef. Peel and chop the onions. Melt the dripping in a heavy-based pan over medium heat. Add the onions and cook for 5 minutes or until just translucent. Stir in the flour and reduce the heat to low.

2 Stir in the stock and wine, and season to taste. Peel and crush the garlic clove and add to the sauce with the bay leaf. Bring to the boil. Simmer for 15 minutes. Remove from the heat and allow to cool. When cool, add the slices of beef. Return to medium heat and simmer for about 10 minutes.

3 Slice the potatoes thinly. Arrange the slices in a ring around the edge of an ovenproof dish. Arrange the slices of beef in the centre. Remove the bay leaf from the sauce and spoon it over the beef. Sprinkle the breadcrumbs over the top. Brown under a hot grill for 3 minutes and serve at once.

MUSHROOM PIE

SERVES 4–6 · 45 MINS TO PREPARE · 1 HR TOTAL TIME
445 KCAL PER SERVING · SUITABLE FOR VEGETARIANS

3 celery sticks, chopped	2–3tsp lemon juice
1 onion, finely chopped	
50g/2oz butter	**TOPPING**
375g/12oz button mushrooms, halved if large	700g/1^1/2lb potatoes
	6tbls milk
50g/2oz plain flour	60g/2oz butter
2tsp sweet paprika	salt and freshly ground black pepper
1tsp dried thyme	
^{1}/4tsp cayenne pepper	sweet paprika, to sprinkle
300ml/^{1}/2pt milk	

1 Heat the oven to 190°C/375°F/gas 5. Boil the potatoes in salted water for 15 minutes or until tender. Meanwhile, fry the celery and onion in the butter gently for 5 minutes until the onion is translucent. Add the mushrooms and cook for a further 2 minutes.

2 Add the flour and stir in well, then add the paprika, thyme, and cayenne pepper. Remove from the heat and gradually stir in the milk. Return to the heat and simmer, stirring constantly, until the sauce is thickened and smooth. Remove from the heat and stir in the lemon juice. Season with salt to taste and set aside.

3 Drain the potatoes well, and mash with the milk and butter. Season with salt and pepper. Pour the mushroom mixture into an ovenproof dish. Spoon over the mashed potatoes, spreading evenly. Sprinkle with paprika, then bake for 20 minutes. Serve at once.

POTATO & CHEESE BAKE

THE FAMILY WILL NEVER TIRE OF THIS SIMPLE
YET TASTY CHEESE DISH WHICH TAKES VERY
LITTLE TIME TO PREPARE
SERVES 4–6 · 15 MINS TO PREPARE · 45 MINS TOTAL TIME
335 KCAL PER SERVING · SUITABLE FOR VEGETARIANS

900g/2lb potatoes, cut into chunks
125ml/4fl oz fromage frais
25g/1oz butter, plus extra for greasing
6tbls Parmesan cheese, grated
salt and freshly ground black pepper
4tbls Edam cheese, grated

1 Heat the oven to 190°C/375°F/gas 5. Place the potatoes in a large saucepan, cover with cold water and cook for 15–20 minutes or until tender. Drain the cooked potatoes thoroughly, then return them to a dry pan and toss briefly over low heat until the remaining moisture evaporates. Mash or process the potatoes to a smooth purée.

2 Add the fromage frais, the butter and grated Parmesan cheese to the potatoes and season with salt and pepper to taste. Spoon the potato mixture into a buttered ovenproof dish and sprinkle with grated Edam. Bake for 25 minutes or until heated through.

INGREDIENTS GUIDE

Edam cheese forms a waxy, bubbly layer on top of the potatoes. Use a different cheese, if you prefer: Gruyère has a strong, very characteristic flavour; Lancashire is mild and melts very quickly; mozzarella has a lovely stringy texture.

COOK'S TIPS

The leftovers from minced beef dishes, such as bolognese sauce or chili con carne add extra flavour to this dish. Put a layer of cooked meat in the base of the dish, then add the potatoes, or stir into the potato before baking the dish in the oven.
When fresh sage is available, stir a few chopped leaves into the mixture before baking, or use some as a garnish.

CELERY & POTATO BAKE

SERVES 4 · 15 MINS TO PREPARE · 1¹/2 HRS TOTAL TIME
420 KCAL PER SERVING · SUITABLE FOR VEGETARIANS

450g/1lb potatoes, cut into
   6mm/¹/4in slices
salt
1tbls vegetable oil
1 bunch of celery, cut into
   12mm/¹/2in slices
225g/¹/2lb French beans
1tbls soy sauce
25g/1oz butter, melted

ALMOND SAUCE
25g/1oz butter
50g/2oz flaked almonds
25g/1oz flour
425ml/³/4pt milk

1 Heat the oven to 190°C/375°F/gas 5. Put the potatoes into a large pan of salted water and bring to the boil. Cover and simmer for 5 minutes. Leave the potatoes in the water and set aside.

2 Meanwhile, heat the oil in a saucepan over medium heat and fry the celery and French beans for 3 minutes or until soft. Add the soy sauce, reduce the heat to low, cover and simmer for 10 minutes.

3 To make the almond sauce, heat the butter in a saucepan over low heat and fry the almonds for 1 minute or until golden. Sprinkle on the flour and stir well for 1 minute. Increase the heat to medium and gradually add the milk, stirring constantly until the sauce boils and thickens. Simmer over low heat for 5 minutes, stirring frequently.

4 Drain the potatoes. Put the celery and beans in a 1.7L/3pt ovenproof dish and pour the almond sauce over the top. Arrange the potato slices over the vegetables and brush with melted butter. Bake for 45 minutes or until browned. Serve at once.

SERVING SUGGESTIONS

Although this is an ideal vegetarian main dish, Celery & Potato Bake can also be served as a side dish for six along with plainly cooked meat, poultry or fish.

WHAT TO DRINK

The crisp, round notes of a Cape Chardonnay from South Africa would be a good match for this tasty dish.

have drained completely, spread them out on pieces of kitchen towel to dry.

3 Melt the butter in a large saucepan, then stir in the garlic, thyme and potato slices. Mix well, then add the beans, tomatoes and sweetcorn, tossing carefully to mix without breaking up the potatoes. Season with salt and pepper to taste.

4 Heat the oven to 230°C/450°F/gas 8. Lightly grease an oven-proof baking dish. Spoon the vegetable mixture into the dish.

5 Bake for 40 minutes, then sprinkle the cheese over the top and bake the dish for a further 10–15 minutes or until bubbling hot and just beginning to brown. Serve at once.

BEAN, SWEETCORN & POTATO BAKE

THIS WARMING VEGETARIAN BAKE IS SURE
TO BECOME A FIRM FAMILY FAVOURITE
SERVES 4 · 40 MINS TO PREPARE · 12 HRS TOTAL TIME WITH SOAKING
450 KCAL PER SERVING · SUITABLE FOR VEGETARIANS

**100g/4oz red kidney beans, soaked
  overnight, or a 400g/14oz tin, drained**
450g/1lb potatoes, peeled
50g/2oz butter, melted
2 garlic cloves
1tsp thyme

400g/14oz tin chopped tomatoes
**75g/3oz frozen sweetcorn kernels,
  defrosted and drained**
salt and freshly ground black pepper
oil for greasing
150g/5oz red Leicester cheese, grated

1 If using dried kidney beans, drain them and put them in a large saucepan with enough fresh water to cover. Bring to the boil and boil vigorously for 15 minutes. Reduce the heat slightly and cook for a further 15–20 minutes until the beans are tender, adding a little salt during the last 5 minutes of the cooking time. Drain and set aside.

2 Using a very sharp knife, cut the potatoes into wafer-thin slices and put them in a colander. Rinse them under cold running water then leave them to drain. When they

SERVING SUGGESTIONS

Serve this bake with new season purple sprouting broccoli, buttered steamed spinach or spring greens.

INGREDIENTS GUIDE

If you haven't much time, use tinned kidney beans in water instead of the dried variety. You only need to rinse them and they are ready to use, thereby cutting out the overnight soaking time and reducing the cooking time of this meal by 35 minutes.

TRADITIONAL LANCASHIRE HOTPOT

SERVES 4 · 25 MINS TO PREPARE
3 HRS TOTAL TIME · 450 KCAL PER SERVING

butter for greasing
700g/1¹/2lb potatoes, thinly sliced
salt and freshly ground black pepper
700g/1¹/2lb middle neck lamb chops, trimmed
2 lamb's kidneys, trimmed and quartered
100g/4oz mushrooms, cut into quarters
1 onion, thinly sliced
300ml/¹/2pt lamb stock, made with 1 stock cube
15g/¹/2oz melted butter

1 Heat the oven to 150°C/300°F/gas 2. Grease a 1.4–1.7L/2¹/2–3pt casserole dish with butter. Put half the potatoes in a layer on the bottom of the prepared dish and season with salt and pepper to taste. Arrange the chops on top of the potatoes and season lightly with salt and pepper. Cover with the kidneys and mushrooms. Season and scatter with the onions. Finish with a layer of the remaining potatoes.

2 Pour in the stock around the sides of the dish and brush the melted butter over the top of the potatoes. Sprinkle lightly with salt. Cover the hotpot and cook in the oven for 1¹/2 hours. Remove the lid and cook for a further hour or until the meat is tender and the potato topping is crisp and golden brown. Serve hot.

FARMHOUSE POTATO BAKE

SERVES 4-6 · 20 MINS TO PREPARE · 1HR 50 MINS TOTAL TIME
425 KCAL PER SERVING · SUITABLE FOR VEGETARIANS

900g/2lb potatoes
25g/1oz margarine
225g/¹/2lb leeks, trimmed and sliced
440g tin condensed mushroom soup
175g/6fl oz sour cream
1tsp dried mixed herbs
salt and freshly ground black pepper
margarine, for greasing
chopped fresh parsley, to garnish

1 Heat the oven to 190°C/375°F/gas 5 and grease a large ovenproof baking dish. Cut the potatoes into 5mm/¹/4in slices and set aside. Melt the margarine in a frying pan, add the leeks and fry gently for 5 minutes until soft. Remove from the heat.

2 In a large bowl, beat the mushroom soup and sour cream together. Add the herbs and salt and pepper to taste, then gently stir in the potatoes and leeks to coat thoroughly.

3 Turn the potato mixture into the greased dish, cover with foil and bake in the oven for 1 hour. Remove the foil and bake for a further 30 minutes until the potatoes are tender. Sprinkle with the chopped parsley and serve straight from the dish.

POTATO & MUSHROOM BAKE

THIS FILLING POTATO DISH IS GOOD ON ITS
OWN OR CAN BE MADE MORE SUBSTANTIAL IF
SERVED WITH GRILLED BACON OR CHOPS,
BAKED BEANS AND CRUSTY FRENCH BREAD
SERVES 4 · 30 MINS TO PREPARE · 1 HR TOTAL TIME
225 KCAL PER SERVING · SUITABLE FOR VEGETARIANS

700g/1 1/2lb potatoes, halved
salt
2tbls vegetable oil
50g/2oz margarine or butter
100g/4oz button mushrooms, thinly sliced
1tsp dried mixed herbs
freshly ground black pepper
2 large tomatoes, sliced

1 Heat the oven to 200°C/400°F/gas 6. Put the potatoes in a large saucepan with cold salted water to
cover, bring to the boil and boil gently for 5 minutes. Drain
the potatoes and allow to cool.

2 Meanwhile, heat the oil and half the margarine in a
saucepan, add the mushrooms and toss them over
moderate heat for about 3 minutes, until they have
absorbed most of the fat. Remove the mushrooms with a
slotted spoon.

3 Slice the potatoes so that they are no thicker than
2mm/1/8in. Grease a shallow ovenproof dish with the
fat remaining in the saucepan. Arrange half the potatoes
overlapping on the base of the dish. Cover with the mushrooms, sprinkle over half the herbs and season the vegetables well with salt and pepper.

4 Arrange the remaining potatoes in a layer to cover
the mushrooms, then arrange the sliced tomatoes on
top. Sprinkle them with the remaining herbs. Melt the
remaining margarine and pour it over the dish.

5 Bake the dish in the centre of the oven for 40–45
minutes, until the potatoes are tender when pierced
with a fine skewer. Serve very hot, straight from the dish.

VERSATILE VEGETABLE HOTPOT

SIMPLE AND INEXPENSIVE TO MAKE, THIS WARMING DISH MAKES THE MOST OF ROOT VEGETABLES AVAILABLE YEAR ROUND

SERVES 4–6
15 MINS TO PREPARE
1¼ HRS TOTAL TIME
310 KCAL PER SERVING
SUITABLE FOR VEGETARIANS

**50g/2oz butter, plus extra for greasing
1tbls vegetable oil
1 garlic clove, chopped
1 large onion, thinly sliced
4 large carrots, thinly sliced
2 celery sticks, sliced
salt and and freshly ground pepper
700g/1½lb potatoes
½ vegetable stock cube
150ml/¼pt boiling water
chopped fresh parsley, to garnish**

1 Heat the oven to 190°C/375°F/gas 5. Grease a 1.1L/2pt oven-proof dish with extra butter.

2 In a heavy-based frying pan, heat the oil with half the butter over medium heat. Add the garlic, onion, carrots and celery and fry for about 8 minutes, stirring frequently, until softened and golden but not browned. Season with the salt and pepper to taste.

3 Cut the potatoes into thin slices and put a layer in the bottom of the prepared dish. Using half the fried vegetables, make another layer on top of the potatoes. Repeat with half the remaining potatoes and the remaining fried vegetables, and finish with the rest of the potatoes. Dissolve the vegetable stock cube in the boiling water and pour over the vegetables.

4 Dot the potato topping with the remaining butter. Cover and cook in the oven for 30 minutes. Remove the cover and continue cooking for a further 20 minutes or until the potatoes are soft, golden and slightly crisp at the edges. Serve hot, sprinkled with chopped parsley.

NUTRITION NOTES

Vegetable Hotpot is low in fat and supplies a useful amount of fibre and vitamin C. With a green salad it makes a great vegetarian supper dish for four, or a tasty vegetable accompaniment to plainly cooked meat, fish or poultry. This recipe serves 6 as a vegetable side dish .

WHAT TO DRINK

This is a delicately flavoured vegetable dish so a light red wine would be most suitable. Try an Italian red such as Bardolino, or a red from Valencia in Spain.

POTATO PIZZA

THIS DELICIOUS PIZZA MAKES AN EXCELLENT
SUPPER DISH SERVED WITH A GREEN SALAD
AND FRENCH BREAD
SERVES 4 · 40 MINS TO PREPARE
1 HR 10 MINS TOTAL TIME WITH CHILLING
500 KCAL PER SERVING
SUITABLE FOR VEGETARIANS

100g/4oz self-raising flour
salt
50g/2oz butter
250g/9oz cold mashed
  potatoes
vegetable oil, for greasing

TOPPING
1 tbls vegetable oil
1 large onion, sliced
1 red pepper, deseeded
  and sliced

1 garlic clove, crushed
  (optional)
125g/4oz button mush-
  rooms, sliced
pinch of oregano
2tsp malt vinegar
freshly ground black
  pepper
1 tbls tomato purée
175g/6oz Cheddar
  cheese, sliced

1 Heat the oven to 230°C/450°F/gas 8. Oil a large baking sheet. Make the pizza base: sift the flour and salt
into a large bowl. Add the butter and rub it in with your fin-
gertips until the mixture resembles breadcrumbs, then add
the mashed potatoes and knead the mixture lightly until
smooth. Press the dough into a 25cm/10in round and
refrigerate.

2 Meanwhile, make the topping: heat the oil in a frying
pan, add the onion, red pepper and garlic, if using, and
fry gently for 5 minutes or until the onion is soft and lightly coloured. Remove the pan from the heat and stir in the
mushrooms, oregano, vinegar and salt and pepper to taste.

3 Place the potato base on the baking sheet and spread
the tomato purée over it, then top with the onion
mixture. Arrange the cheese slices over the top. Bake in the
oven for 25–30 minutes or until the base is firm and the
cheese is golden brown.

VARIATIONS
For a more Italian flavour, top the cheese with anchovy fillets,
slices of salami and black olives, then drizzle with a little olive oil
to prevent drying out. Mozzarella cheese can be used instead of
Cheddar.

3 Arrange a layer of potatoes in the bottom of a shallow, well-oiled ovenproof dish. Cover with a layer of tomatoes. Repeat the layering, finishing with a layer of potatoes on the top.

4 Heat the oven to 200°C/400°F/gas 6. Sprinkle the top with the olives and breadcrumbs, then drizzle over the remaining olive oil.

5 Bake the tian in the oven for 15–20 minutes or until the top is crisp and golden. Garnish with bay leaves and an olive before serving.

VARIATIONS

Layer the potatoes and tomatoes with mozzarella rounds, and sprinkle the surface with grated Cheddar or Parmesan cheese.

SERVING SUGGESTIONS

Serve this dish on its own with a simple green salad, or as an accompaniment to a roast, or Provençal-style stew.

WHAT TO DRINK

This herby potato dish can take the full body of a local red wine such as Bandol. A lighter choice is Sillon de Palère rosé.

POTATO & TOMATO TIAN

THIS SUSTANTIAL PROVENÇAL DISH IS FRAGRANT WITH HERBS AND FRUITY OLIVE OIL. IT IS TRADITIONALLY BAKED IN A TIAN, OR CLAY DISH
SERVES 6 · 35 MINS TO PREPARE · 1 HR 10 MINS TOTAL TIME
345 KCAL PER SERVING · SUITABLE FOR VEGETARIANS

1kg/2¹/4lb potatoes, unpeeled
5tbls extra virgin olive oil
1tbls finely chopped rosemary
2–3 fresh bay leaves, cut into thin strips lengthways
salt and freshly ground black pepper

6 tomatoes, sliced
10 oil-cured black olives, pitted and chopped
50g/2oz fresh breadcrumbs
bay leaves and an olive, to garnish

1 Boil the potatoes for 10–15 minutes until just tender. Drain, then remove the skins when the potatoes are cool enough to handle. Cut the potatoes into thick slices and put them in a bowl.

2 Pour 4 tablespoons of the olive oil over the potatoes and add the rosemary and bay leaves. Season with salt and black pepper to taste, then toss gently with wooden spoons, taking care not to break up the potato slices too much.

INGREDIENTS GUIDE

Canadian Cheddar cheese has just the right amount of flavour to give a kick to the potatoes and cabbage.

COOK'S TIPS

To see if the underside of the bubble and squeak is golden brown, gently lift up the edge with a palette knife. The centre will become brown before the outside, so take care not to let the centre burn.

CHEESY BUBBLE & SQUEAK

LIKE MANY DISHES ORIGINALLY DEVISED FOR USING UP LEFTOVERS, BUBBLE AND SQUEAK IS GOOD ENOUGH TO MAKE FROM SCRATCH FOR ITS OWN SAKE

SERVES 4 · 20 MINS TO PREPARE
50 MINS TOTAL TIME · 510 KCAL PER SERVING

900g/2lb potatoes, quartered
salt
450g/1lb green cabbage, cored and shredded
175g/6oz mature Cheddar cheese, grated
1 large egg, beaten
freshly ground black pepper
6–8 spring onions, chopped
25g/1oz dripping or lard

1 Cook the potatoes in boiling salted water for 20 minutes or until tender. Meanwhile, cook the cabbage in boiling salted water for 5 minutes and drain it thoroughly.

2 Drain the potatoes well, then return them to the saucepan. Dry out over gentle heat, then mash with 100g/4oz cheese, the beaten egg and plenty of salt and pepper. Stir in the cabbage and spring onions.

3 Melt the dripping in a large frying pan over high heat and swirl it around to cover the base and sides. Add the bubble and squeak mixture and spread it out evenly. Cook for 3 minutes or until the underside is golden.

4 Sprinkle with the remaining cheese, then put under a moderate grill for about 5 minutes or until the top is golden brown. Cut into wedges and serve at once straight from the pan.

VARIATIONS

Traditional bubble and squeak is made with left-over mashed potato and cooked Brussels sprouts. If you prefer the stronger flavour of sprouts, then use these instead of the cabbage. A dash of Worcestershire sauce is a good complement to the cheese. Add it when mashing the potatoes and, if liked, mix a few drops in with the grated cheese for the topping.

BUBBLE & SQUEAK WITH SUN-DRIED TOMATOES

SUN-DRIED TOMATOES GIVE THIS OLD-FASHIONED DISH,
TRADITIONALLY A WAY OF USING UP LEFTOVER VEGETABLES, A PIQUANCY
THAT TRANSFORMS IT INTO A MOUTH-WATERING MEAL
SERVES 4 · 20 MINS TO PREPARE · 45 MINS TOTAL TIME · 225 KCAL PER SERVING
SUITABLE FOR VEGETARIANS

6 sun-dried tomatoes
**2tbls oil (you can use the oil from
   the tomatoes)**
25g/1oz butter
**1 bunch spring onions, sliced
   diagonally**

1tsp caraway seeds
**150g/5oz raw spring greens or cabbage,
   finely shredded**
**700g/1¹/2lb cooked potatoes, roughly
   mashed**
salt and freshly ground black pepper

1 Soak the tomatoes if using dried, or lift out of the oil, and slice finely. Heat the oil and butter together in a large, heavy-based frying pan or wok over medium-high heat. Add the spring onions and caraway seeds and fry for 2–3 minutes, stirring constantly. Add the greens and stir-fry for about 10 minutes or until the vegetables are nearly cooked.

2 Add the potatoes, mashing so that the vegetables are well mixed. Stir in the tomatoes. Add salt and freshly ground black pepper to taste.

3 Press down to form a cake, then reduce the heat and cook for 20 minutes or until the base is crusty. Heat the grill so that you can finish the cake by browning it under the grill for 2–5 minutes. Cut into wedges to serve.

WHAT TO DRINK
Everyone loves this homely dish. Eat it with a glass of inexpensive Shiraz/Cabernet Sauvignon blend from Australia.

INGREDIENTS GUIDE
Sun-dried tomatoes are available loose or packed in oil. If you buy them in oil you can use them straight from the jar. If they are dry, cover them with hot water and set aside for at least an hour before using. Drain well before adding to dishes.

VARIATIONS
For an all-in-one meal, include bacon or ham in this dish. If you are using bacon, allow a couple of rashers per person. Grill the bacon until crisp, then crumble it on to kitchen towel and keep warm. Stir into the potato and cabbage with the sun-dried tomatoes. If you are using ham, cut it into narrow strips and add it to the pan with the tomatoes.

BUBBLE & SQUEAK WITH BACON

SERVES 4 · 20 MINS TO PREPARE
50 MINS TOTAL TIME · 465 KCAL PER SERVING

4tbls olive oil
1 Spanish onion, finely
  chopped
100g/4oz lean, streaky
  bacon, coarsely chopped
2 garlic cloves, crushed
900g/2lb potatoes, cooked
  and mashed
450g/1lb cabbage, cooked
and coarsely chopped
1tsp Worcestershire
  sauce
salt and freshly ground
  black pepper
50g/2oz butter, cut into
  small pieces
finely chopped parsley to
  garnish (optional)

1 In a large heavy-based frying pan, heat the olive oil. Sauté the onion and bacon until the onion is golden brown and the bacon crisp, turning occasionally with a wooden spoon. Add the crushed garlic and mix well.

2 Combine the mashed potatoes and the chopped cooked cabbage. Season with Worcestershire sauce, salt and pepper, then add the butter. Mix the potato and cabbage well with the sautéed onion and bacon in the frying pan. Pat the mixture into a cake and fry over a steady heat for 4–5 minutes, or until the bottom of the cake is brown and crisp.

3 Turn the cake on to a flat plate, then slip it back into the pan to cook on the other side for the same length of time. Sprinkle with finely chopped parsley and serve.

CARROT & POTATO SOUFFLÉ

SERVES 4 · 40 MINS TO PREPARE · 1¼ HRS TOTAL TIME
380 KCAL PER SERVING · SUITABLE FOR VEGETARIANS

450g/1lb carrots, cut into
  2.5cm/1in pieces
350g/12oz potatoes, cut
  into 2.5cm/1in pieces
salt
25g/1oz butter
2tbls milk
4–5tsp French mustard
100g/4oz mature
  Cheddar cheese, grated
5 eggs, separated
freshly ground black
  pepper
margarine, for greasing

1 Heat the oven to 200°C/400°F/gas 6. Grease a 1.5L/2½pt soufflé dish. Bring the carrots to the boil in a large saucepan of salted water, reduce the heat and cook for about 15 minutes or until tender. Cook the potatoes in the same way for about 10 minutes or until tender.

2 Drain the cooked vegetables and transfer to a clean saucepan. Mash with the butter and milk until smooth. Transfer to a large bowl and mix in the mustard, cheese, egg yolks and salt and pepper to taste. Beat with a wooden spoon until smooth.

3 In a clean dry bowl, whisk the egg whites until stiff but not dry. Using a large metal spoon, fold them lightly into the carrot and potato mixture. Pour into the prepared dish and bake in theve at once.

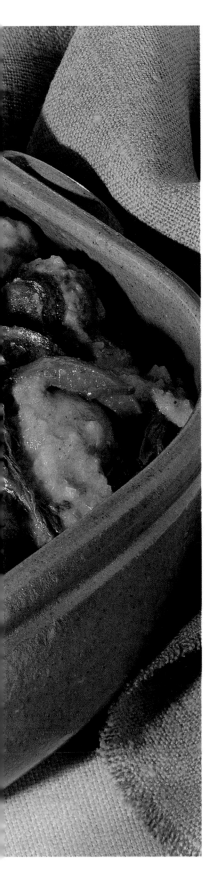

SPICY VEGETABLE BALTI

THIS COLOURFUL VEGETABLE DISH IS DELICIOUSLY SPICY AND FULL OF INTERESTING TEXTURES. MAKE THE BALTI SAUCE IN ADVANCE AND THE DISH TAKES ONLY MINUTES TO COOK
SERVES 4–6 · 35 MINS TO PREPARE · 1 HR 25 MINS TOTAL TIME
360 KCAL PER SERVING · SUITABLE FOR VEGETARIANS

BALTI SAUCE
1¹/2 large Spanish onions, chopped
2¹/2tbls ghee or vegetable oil
2 garlic cloves, crushed
25mm/1in fresh root ginger, peeled and chopped
³/4tsp fenugreek seeds
³/4tsp ground coriander
³/4tsp cumin
¹/2tsp fennel seeds
¹/2tsp turmeric
pinch chilli powder
seeds from 3 cardamom pods
2¹/2 pieces cassia bark
1–2 cinnamon sticks, depending on size
200ml/7fl oz stock or water
3 chopped tomatoes
2 bay leaves

VEGETABLES
700g/1¹/2lb spinach, stalks removed
2 potatoes, peeled and cut into small pieces
salt
boiling water
4tbls ghee or vegetable oil
1tsp cumin seeds
1tsp fenugreek seeds
1tsp ground turmeric
2tsp garam masala
¹/4–¹/2tsp chilli powder
1 onion, quartered and thinly sliced
2 garlic cloves, crushed
1 large red pepper, de-seeded and cut into 6mm/¹/4in strips
450g/1lb button mushrooms

1 First make the sauce: stir-fry the onions in the ghee, or vegetable oil, until translucent. Add the garlic and all the spices and stir together. Add the stock, or water, tomatoes and bay leaves. Bring to the boil, then reduce the heat, cover and simmer for 25 minutes, stirring often. Discard the cassia and bay leaves, cool slightly and purée in a blender or food processor.

2 Wash the spinach and place in a large saucepan with only the water clinging to the leaves. Cover and cook over medium heat for 5 minutes or until it is wilted, turning frequently. Drain well in a colander, pressing firmly with the back of a spoon to extract as much liquid as possible. Cook the potatoes in a pan of salted boiling water for about 8 minutes or until just tender. Drain well.

3 Heat the ghee or oil in a balti pan, wok or large, deep frying pan over medium heat. Add the spices and stir-fry for 30 seconds. Add the onion, garlic and red pepper and stir-fry for 2 minutes. Add the mushrooms and continue stir-frying for a further 2–3 minutes.

4 Stir in the potato pieces, spinach, salt to taste and the prepared balti sauce, using two forks to separate any thick clumps of spinach leaves. Cook gently for 3 minutes or until heated through. Transfer to a serving dish and serve hot.

COOK'S TIPS
The cooked spinach may be coarsely chopped, if wished, although the appearance is better if left as whole leaf spinach. Make sure that the spinach is thoroughly drained after cooking or the excess liquid will make the consistency of the finished dish rather thin and watery.
To speed up the cooking process for future balti meals, why not make double the quantity of Balti sauce in advance and freeze what you don't need now, ready to use when required?

WHAT TO DRINK
Red wine goes well with spicy foods, so try a young beaujolais with this balti meal. However, if you don't want to drink wine, then a chilled Indian lager or pilsner beer would be ideal.

INDEX